TWO TEENAGERS IN TWENTY

Two Teenagers in Twenty

Writings by gay & lesbian youth

edited by ANN HERON

Boston ♦ Alyson Publications, Inc.

If you found this book, it's dedicated to you.

Published by Alyson Publications, Inc.,
40 Plympton Street, Boston, Massachusetts 02118.
Distributed in England by GMP Publishers,
P.O. Box 247, London N17 9QR, England.

First edition: June 1994

ISBN 1-55583-229-6

5   4   3   2   1

Stories that begin on the following pages are reprinted from the original
edition of *One Teenager in Ten.*: 19, 23, 28, 37, 44, 52, 57, 68, 75, 78, 81, 85, 89,
101, 104, 110, 118, 122, 127, 134, 137, 150, 152, 170. Other stories are original
to this new book.

Library of Congress Cataloging-in-Publication Data

Two teenagers in twenty : writings by gay and lesbian youth / edited
    by Ann Heron. — 1st ed.
        p.   cm.
    ISBN 1-55583-229-6 (cloth) : $17.95
    1. Gay teenagers—United States—Case studies—Juvenile
literature. [1. Homosexuality.] I. Heron, Ann. II. Title: 2
teenagers in 20.
HQ76.3.U5T96   1994
305.9'0664'0835—dc20   94-9761
                                                              CIP
                                                              AC

Contents

Introduction

In March of 1980, Alyson Publications issued the book *Young, Gay and Proud!* In the back, the publisher announced plans for a second book, consisting of first-person stories written by lesbian and gay youth, and asked teenagers to contribute. I was working at Alyson at the time, and was happy to take on the project of pulling all these contributions into a cohesive book. For three years I solicited more essays, and worked with contributors as they revised their stories. Finally, *One Teenager in Ten* was published. The title referred to common estimates that about one-tenth of the population is gay.

The world changed dramatically in the decade that followed. Lesbians and gay men became far more visible in the media, a visibility that reached its peak in the debate about gays in the military. The nightmare of AIDS forced many people to address gay issues for the first time, and created new concerns for teenagers who were just coming out. A decade after *One Teenager in Ten* first appeared, publisher Sasha Alyson and I agreed that it was time to reflect these changes in a new edition.

For two years, I sought out stories from a new generation of lesbian and gay youth. I found some of them through the free penpal service that Alyson Publications provided following publication of *One Teenager in Ten;* others responded to notices in gay newspapers. I dropped a few stories from the original book and added nineteen new ones, nearly doubling the length of the first edition. (Those who want to know which stories appeared in the original edition and which were written more recently may refer to the copyright page.) This new book, I believe, gives a realistic sense of what life is like for gay and lesbian teenagers.

Early in the process, we agreed on the title *Two Teenagers in Twenty* for this new edition. It was clear that more and more teenagers were identifying themselves as gay or lesbian, often at an increasingly younger age. The new title would reflect that reality.

We originally hoped the new title could also symbolize another change: that it was easier now for gay young people to find one another. Unfortunately, that was not the case. There's been some growth in support groups available to gay teenagers, but it hasn't kept pace with the number of teens who are confronting issues of sexual orientation. The sense of isolation and despair in the stories I received in 1993 was in fact even stronger than a decade ago.

To me, that isolation emphasizes the irrelevance of the debate over the estimate that one-tenth of the population is gay. (This figure was derived from the work of researcher Alfred C. Kinsey, who estimated in 1948 that 10 percent of the white male population was more or less exclusively homosexual for at least three years between the ages of 16 and 55.) One recent and widely publicized study claimed that only 1 or 2 percent of the population is gay, though the researchers later acknowledged that their survey methods may have yielded inaccurate information. Other studies have come up with estimates ranging from 2 to 10 percent. The fact is, as long as people can lose jobs, friends, and even family because they are gay, it will be nearly impossible to come up with an accurate figure.

The exact percentage isn't important. What matters is that we, as a society, are failing to provide critical information and support for young people who feel they may be different. That failure cries out from nearly every story in this book.

If you're one of those young people, I hope these stories will show that you're not alone; other teenagers have gone through experiences much like yours. If you're an adult, I hope that after reading this book you'll look for ways to provide the support that gay teenagers need. In either case, this collection is a start; at the back of the book, you'll find suggestions and guidelines for taking the next step.

Ann Heron

Rachel Corbett, 16

Madison, Wisconsin

Throughout and since childhood, I've been a "tomboy." In my second-grade picture, I was wearing a plaid shirt with rainbow suspenders and jeans. I hated dresses and nylons. I thought they were uncomfortable and never understood why I should have to wear uncomfortable clothes. My hair has almost always been cut short. Once, I tried to grow it out, only to get sick of it and chop it off. To this day, I've had more male friends than female friends. As a child, I chose the He-Man figurine or Matchbox cars over the Strawberry Shortcake doll or Barbie. I was always outside on my dirt bike skinning my knees instead of inside playing house.

My mother had a couple of gay and lesbian friends when I was growing up. That's the first place I learned about being gay or lesbian. When I was young, I don't think I saw any difference between heterosexual and homosexual relationships. I was young and was brought up to believe love is love, whether it involves people of the opposite sex or people of the same sex. It wasn't until I started Catholic school in the sixth grade that I became aware of homophobia. Kids would always make comments about effeminate men and say that all the nuns at the school were lesbians. It was at that school where I learned that there is a great deal of opposition to homosexuality.

That same year, some new people moved into the neighborhood. After they had settled in, I went over to see if they had any children I could be friends with. Luckily for me, they had two boys. They were a little younger than me, but I wasn't about to be fussy. (Most of the other kids in my neighborhood were either infants or in high school.) The boys in the house were being raised by two women. As time went on, I realized that they were probably lesbians. The two women never told me that they were gay, and neither did their sons. When they moved in, the boys were about seven and eight, and I'm not sure if they knew about their moms. I can understand why the women wouldn't tell me. I was eleven at the time, and they probably weren't sure what my parents would think. I'm pretty sure they were gay, though: they shared a bedroom, and one time I heard them talking about the bills together. The boys' dads were the only men I ever saw around the place. (And recently, I saw the two women at a documentary about lesbians; I guess that pretty much confirms it!)

The two women and their children made me aware of a new type of lifestyle that I really hadn't known existed. I began to realize that I wanted to live a life like theirs ... not like the one my parents lived. Before they moved in, I could never picture myself being a housewife while my husband went out and earned the money for our family. I realized that I could relate more to them than to my parents. Over the years, I have lost touch with them, and I regret that. But they are still very important role models in my life. They made me aware of my sexual orientation, and I thank them.

Last October, I was downtown walking around with a friend. We saw all these people marching down State Street chanting. One chant went like this: "Two, four, six, eight, how do you know your mother's straight?" I asked my friend what was going on. She told me it was a gay pride march. We watched for a while, and I was so happy to see gays, lesbians, and bisexuals unafraid to show their affection for one another. They were standing up for their rights and demanding more. That night I returned home feeling very proud and decided that it was time for me to come out to my mother.

I was scared about what my mother would say. I was worried that she wouldn't accept me. I knew she supported homosexual rights, because whenever hatemongers were on the talk shows saying that homosexuals should be killed, my mother stood up for the homosexuals. She even yelled obscenities at the TV screen! But even though I knew she was for homosexual rights, I wasn't sure how she'd feel about her daughter being a lesbian. She had always talked about me having a big marriage ceremony in a Catholic church, and a huge reception with a big cake. I didn't want to disappoint her; I wanted to live up to all the expectations I thought she had of me. After thinking about it, I realized that it wouldn't be fair for me to hide my sexual orientation from her. After all, she was my best friend and she should be able to accept it. She had always been there for me no matter what, and I hoped she still would be after I told her.

That night, I was feeling bold, so I started on my way up the stairs to her bedroom. I went in and sat on her bed like I've done many times before when I had something to talk about. She sat up and asked, "What's up, kiddo?" I sat in the dark silence. I tried to speak, but instead I began to cry.

"Rachel, what's the matter? I can't help you unless you tell me what's wrong."

I looked her in the eyes, wishing she could read my mind. It would be so much simpler that way. No chance of that happening. I began to cry harder and wanted to back down.

But there was no way I could just tell her that I'd had a nightmare. I had to tell her the truth; I had to get it over with.

"Mom?"

"Yes, Rachel. Go ahead. You can tell me anything."

"Mom." Tears rolled down my face. "Mom, I'm..."

"Go ahead, honey, it's okay."

"Mom..." I took a deep breath and decided this was it. "I'm a ... a ... a ... lesbian." I cried again.

"Go ahead, honey. Tell me the rest. You can trust me."

"Mom, that's it. I'm a lesbian."

"So why are you so upset?"

"I thought you would be upset, because I'm never going to have a husband and a big wedding."

Mom began to chuckle as she surrounded me with a hug. "I'm so proud of you." A tear rolled down her cheek. "You're my daughter and I love you. I will always love you, no matter what you are. I will always support you in everything that you do. As long as you're happy, I'm happy. You sure are silly, though," she said to me with a smile on her face.

I smiled and began to cry again, because I was filled with so much joy. We talked for a long time. She asked me if I minded if anyone else in our house knew. I told her it would be okay with me, and within three days my father, grandmother, and brother knew. They all took it very well. They are proud of me.

In the weeks that followed, my mother and I talked more than ever before. She was and still is extremely supportive of me. I thank her so much. If she didn't accept me, I don't know if I'd still be around.

Now, at the age of sixteen — one year after coming out to my mother, and many books and movies later — I have learned a lot more about myself. If I had a choice, I wouldn't change my sexual orientation. I am angry, because I find it hard to meet other gays my age. But in a year and a half, I will be in college and there will be more people to meet.

Inside, I'm proud of what I am, but I'm not out to the general public. I believe that coming out is an ongoing process. Since I've told my mother, I've also told a few close friends. I have begun to speak up for homosexual rights in my private Catholic school and soon will deal with gay issues in my photography. I've also spoken to groups about what it's like to be a gay teenager. In college I'm hoping I'll be able to step further and further out of the closet, because I'll be in a more diverse group of people. And, hopefully, they will be more accepting than the five hundred students at my school.

So far, my coming-out experiences have been very positive. Again, I would like to express my thanks to the two women on the corner raising their sons, and to my best friend, who happens to be my mother. I admire you all.

Kyle Dale Bynion, 18

Baltimore, Maryland

All my life I've known I was different. But if someone were to ask me *how* I feel different, I wouldn't be able to answer them. The best way to explain it would be to say that being attracted to the same sex is as natural to me as being attracted to the opposite sex is for heterosexuals.

I have probably known I was gay since I was twelve. I don't think I knew that there *was* such a thing as "gay" until then. I used to go down in the cellar with other boys. We'd touch and kiss each other. I know it's natural for children to "experiment" with the same sex, but I knew, even then, that that was what I wanted. When I finally figured out what I was, I honestly don't remember feeling any different. I guess being gay just felt natural to me. Of course, I didn't realize back then how hard and frustrating it was going to be.

I have a twin brother, Chad, who is also gay. I figured out Chad was gay at about the same time I figured myself out. I don't remember how I knew. I just knew. When I was seventeen, I came out to my brother and his lover. We were all away on vacation. They were in bed, and I just came in and blurted it all out. I'd known about them for a long time, but they had no clue that I was gay. I'd been very active sexually since I was twelve, and I had lots of stories to tell them. I felt great. And, of course, nothing changed between us.

Then my parents found out about Chad. My mother found a letter from his lover in his drawer. They were devastated. My mother wondered what she'd done wrong. She was afraid my little sister would be a lesbian. My stepfather immediately suspected that I was gay too. At the time, I wasn't ready to admit it to them, so I adamantly denied it. But my stepfather wouldn't stop harassing me. Finally, I just yelled, "Shut up! I'm gay. You're right!" Finally. It was off my chest and I felt good.

But two weeks later, I found out my mom thought I was kidding. She hadn't thought I meant it. When I saw the hope in her eyes, I couldn't tell her that I'd been serious. She'd be crushed. I decided I'd tell her after she accepted my brother.

In the meantime, I made a mistake. I told someone I thought I could trust about me and Chad. It turned out he wasn't really a friend. He told everyone. All of our friends at work found out. Chad felt a lot of resentment toward me.

Then my mom found out about me. Apparently, she went through my drawers and found some gay literature. She confronted me, and I told her the truth. I thought it would feel great to have this burden off my shoulders, but it didn't. It did feel good that I didn't have to hide anymore. But her heart was broken. She blamed herself, my father, me. I tried to convince her that it's no one's fault. But she was too wrapped up in her religion to listen to me. She thought her prayers could make me straight.

I was a wreck. I began considering suicide. Just the thought of me tormenting her for the rest of her life tore me up inside. I didn't know if I was strong enough to handle it. I never wanted to hurt her.

I have often been asked (or overheard others being asked, about themselves) if I would go "straight" if I could. Though I have never honestly answered them, I'd like to now. If I could change my sexuality, I would. I know I'll probably offend a lot of people by saying that, but let me explain. My family has literally been uprooted by this. I know that my brother and I, and our friends, and everyone else has a right to be gay and enjoy anything that a heterosexual would. It shouldn't matter whom we go to bed with, but it does. That is why I would change my sexuality if I could – because I don't like hurting people I love. But I can't. And I'm not going to suppress my wants and desires just to please some narrow-minded people.

Thank you for giving me and others an opportunity to express ourselves. In this world where gays are so oppressed, it's good to be able to have a voice.

Gretchen Anthony, 17

New Hampshire

I guess my life has always been rough, but the last two years have been the worst, because that's when I began coming out to myself, a few friends, and, most recently, to my mother.

Nine years ago, I had my first big crush, on a girl I met in Girl Scout Camp. Her name was Terri F., and she came from another town in New Hampshire. In camp, we held hands — at the time, I must have thought nothing of it. She was the most beautiful girl I had ever seen, and I worshipped her. We left camp, and up until recently (two years ago), that's all I could remember of her. For eight years, I thought of a girl named Terri.

My grammar school days were otherwise "normal." In eighth grade, I liked a boy named Phillip and eagerly pursued him. But when I was unsuccessful, it was no big deal. My first two years of high school weren't so easy. I'm not very pretty, and not one boy in that whole school of twelve hundred kids liked me. I began picking beautiful girlfriends and writing poems about them. I wasn't really upset that none of the guys liked me. I was pleased that I had so many girlfriends and got along with them.

Then, during my junior year, I ran into Terri again, one night at a winter track meet. I was watching this girl run, and I didn't know who she was, but she looked familiar. I asked someone who she was, and they said her name was Terri F. I found out a few other things – just to make sure it was her. And this time I really fell in love with her. I watched her at every track meet and got the same funny feeling in my stomach. Sometimes I would walk over near her to see if she remembered me. She would glance at me and then walk away. I looked her up in the phone book and sent her a letter saying who I was. I got no reply. I discovered she worked at a mall near her town. I started going into the store where she worked. I even talked to her once. Every time I saw her, I thought she was more beautiful than before. I still watch her, and I know I'm in love with her forever whether she knows me or not.

I figured I must be gay, and I began "liking" other girls – friends of mine. But I made a promise to myself that I would never touch one of my close friends – not while I was in high school. So I repressed these feelings. I began feeling crazy, suicidal, and depressed. I kept thinking that, in such a small town, I must be the only gay person. When I could take it no longer, I started telling friends I knew I could trust.

The first person I told about my gayness was a friend in my French class. She wasn't my best friend or anyone like that; she was just an average friend. But I knew I had to tell someone, because I was going crazy keeping it to myself. We were coming back from a track meet at the University of New Hampshire, and I felt I had to tell her then. I don't remember being nervous or anything. I just thought to myself, "Well, if she doesn't like it, I have plenty of other friends to fall back on." So we were riding along, and I said, "Nancy, I think I'm gay."

She didn't say anything, and I thought for sure that she was going to stop the car and make me walk. She looked at me and asked, "Have you ever been to bed with a girl?" I said, "No, but..." She cut in, "Well, then, you're just afraid of guys." And she told me all about her boyfriends, and I just sat there. I never brought it up in front of her again.

When I decided to tell my oldest friend, I was really nervous. We were just walking around and I kept trying to bring it up, but I didn't know how and I was afraid of what she would say. At that point, I couldn't deal with the possibility of rejection. Finally, we were on the steps to her house, and I said, "Gayle, I think I'm gay." And she said, "I don't believe you."

I said, "Well, you're going to have to, because I know I'm gay." She didn't say anything, and for a very long time, we weren't able to talk about it. Sometimes she still says she doesn't believe I'm gay, but now we talk about it and she tries to understand.

After that, I came out to various friends, people I knew I could trust or friends I knew would still be friends. Eleven of my straight friends know, and eleven of them have stayed. So far, so good.

Telling my friends helped a little but not much, because even though they somewhat accepted it, they did not want to talk about it. They kept saying they didn't believe me.

Then a family with a boy around my age moved into the neighborhood. Telling myself I didn't want to be gay, I decided to give boys another chance. (I'm not always so thrilled about being gay.) Chuck and I became friends and started doing things together, but we weren't sexually attracted to one another. Before I knew it, we were both coming out to each other at the mall where Terri worked!

I told Chuck because I thought he might be gay too, and because sometimes I can't keep my mouth shut about it. We were sitting in this restaurant, and I kind of whispered, "I'm queer." And he whispered back, "So am I."

Then I stopped whispering. "Are you really?? Tell me more. Do you know any gays around here? When did you first find out? Have you ever had a lover?"

Chuck has been really great for me, because he's my age and I've met some older gays through him. But I still don't know any lesbians, and this drives me crazy.

Chuck also brought me up to a gay bar in Ogunquit, Maine, where I had a blast. Even if you're underage, you can still get into bars. All it takes is brains and plans. Plan A: Know the person at the door. Plan B: Get there early enough that no one is at the door. I've now been to five different bars, and I've gotten in every time.

One day a Boston newspaper ran an article on gay youth. It had information about books and bookstores and an organization for gay and lesbian youth called BAGLY (Boston Alliance of Gay and Lesbian Youth). I kept the paper and wrote down all the important stuff and saved it. On my next trip to Boston, I went right to Glad Day Bookshop and spent twenty dollars on books and bought my first copy of *Gay Community News*.

I finally came out to my mother. She accepted it, but she told me that I have one hell of a life ahead of me. She told me it would be easier if I changed. But I can't change, and I don't want to change. I'm seventeen and a half years old, and I have yet to meet another lesbian. I have my whole life ahead of me ... if I don't go crazy.

Christopher Hawks, 17

New Jersey

I am seventeen years old, a senior in high school, and openly gay. Homosexuality has always been a major force in the shaping of my life and personality. Learning to be myself and to like myself has been a continuous growing experience, one that is still going on.

It is impossible to say just when I first realized I was gay. Looking back, I can see that I have always liked other boys, but it wasn't until I was thirteen that I learned that the name for my passion was "homosexuality."

Even then, I was not ashamed of what I was. I knew I had to be discreet, even though I didn't look like the stereotypical gay. I was never ashamed, but I was embarrassed. Being gay was not popular; it was used as a put-down quite often. So I pretended a little, and withdrew a lot, never knowing if I could ever be myself.

I did have one very short-lived romance in school, but we were doomed from the start: he was too uptight about being gay and I wasn't. But my first real affair was with a much older man, and he was a beautiful person. I grew so much from our relationship. He shared his experience with me, and his love, and I grew. He helped me to like myself as I never had. I felt so good about myself and being myself that I decided that no one was going to force me to be someone else. Thus, I began to come out.

My first step was to tell a close friend of mine. After I had told her and found that she still liked me and that my gayness didn't bother her, I decided to tell some more close friends. I eventually told all the people that I cared about, or they found out before I told them. My final step was to pierce my ear; that way anyone who wasn't sure that what they had heard was true could see it for themselves.

I also told my parents. It was a major step for me. My parents had split up, and most of the time I lived in Florida with my mother, but I spent the summers with my father just outside of Philadelphia. As it became more and more apparent that my mother was not going to celebrate my gayness, I became more and more tired of the charade. My one refuge seemed to be the summers, so I turned them into a permanent thing and moved in with my father.

Very little of what I expected to happen happened. My father and I did not get along, but at least our problems did not revolve around my being gay. The best thing that came from my move was that I was now close to a big city. The city is wonderful! There are so many gays everywhere. It made me feel so good to go into the city and see them all living openly and happily, and it gave me strength to be myself.

Being gay hasn't always been easy. As with anything, I've had my share of hassles, but I've learned I must be myself. The times of intimacy and love that can be shared when you are honest are far better than the many times when you pretend to be what you are not.

One recent example occurred on graduation night. Everyone was going to a party somewhere. I showed up a little early for one my friend was having, and and we had some champagne. But that was only the beginning for her. As the night progressed, she got totalled and left her house, with over a hundred people still there partying, to go to another party. So her boyfriend and I took over. I became DJ, and he started to bounce some unwanteds. Pretty soon the party was really jamming. I was dancing and had gotten most everyone up on their feet too, and the party was a smash. Afterwards, some people came up to me and said that they were sorry they had let a stereotype get in the way of getting to know me, and that I was really okay.

Well, after that, I wondered just how many friendships I had lost by not being myself, for surely honesty will make me more popular than any person I could have manufactured and presented.

This was just one of the times I could never have shared had I not begun the lifelong process of coming out, a process that has provided me with a sense of self-worth and self-confidence.

Anonymous, 16

Maine

I'm not exactly sure when I figured out I was gay. It just came naturally, you know. I was feeling things for guys and unexpected things were happening when I looked at guys. I was about eleven or twelve when these feelings started.

I was scared at first, because I was brought up to believe it was a sin and bad or dirty. (Yeah, right.)

▼

I told my younger brother when I was about thirteen. I guess he was the only one I trusted. It was hard. I told him I had something to say to him, but then I couldn't say it. I waited for a week, but he was curious and kept asking me what it was. I finally told him. He was surprised, but he was really too young to understand and didn't say much to me about it. He did tell his friend, though, and that started people talking.

My parents found out and asked me about the "embarrassing rumors" they had heard. I admitted to being gay. They said I'd grow out of it. But I didn't, and soon they realized that I really liked guys. They said that it was not normal, that it was wrong, and that it was a sin. Finally, my parents disowned me and kicked me out, because I hated them and I was so depressed. My sisters and brothers didn't care that I was gay, but most of my aunts and uncles and friends forgot I was alive. Some of my friends found out from my brother, and I told others myself. It was hard. I came to realize that they were not real friends.

Now I live in a residential center for kids. I'm not living at home, because I have no home. It's been two years now, and my parents don't want anything to do with me. I don't want anything to do with them either, but I do wish I had someone who cared for me and loved me for who I am. My brother and I are still in contact with each other. I get a call from him every once in a while. He's a great brother.

▼

I found other gay people by coming out of the closet. By doing that, I found others coming out to me. I have two gay pen pals and a few gay friends now.

AIDS is a big threat to me, but I think a straight guy could get it as easy as a gay guy. I haven't had any sexual contact (yet), but I plan to protect myself.

I'm getting more comfortable with myself, and I'm happy to be who I am. I know what's right for me, and no one can take that away.

David Johnson, 17

Wheeling, West Virginia

When I was fifteen, my brother Troy left home and I inherited his chores and still carried my own. I didn't really mind, because my allowance went up from five to ten dollars a week. Christmas vacation had just ended, as I recall, and I was returning to school. Mother had said I could get my hair styled any way that I wanted, and I had decided on an afro, because I wanted to look like Troy. (I still recall the time I went to school with my hair combed and glasses off and no one knew who I was.) I finally had the money and told Mother I wanted an afro. She hit the roof. I was surprised at the way I reacted, because I never really argued with Mother. But suddenly everything that I had stored up — all my frustrations and hatreds — came pouring out at her. She couldn't handle it, I guess; she expected it from Troy or Korri ... but from me, never!

I stomped into my room, and for three solid hours I sat there brooding. Then, at about eight-thirty, she came in very sober (a sure sign that she had been drinking), and I could tell she had been crying. As in the past, on rare occasions, she asked me if I wanted to see if we could reach my father on the phone. We had been trying to for the last ten years and had never been able to reach him, but this night it was different. We got hold of Grandma Davis and she called Dad, and he called us. Mother talked to him first, and then I talked to him.

Before I knew it, arrangements had been made for me to fly to California and stay with him. But first Mother had made him swear out his address and send a two-way plane ticket. She wanted to make sure that once I got there he didn't take me and vanish.

On a Wednesday evening, I found myself at Tampa airport getting ready to board a plane to San Francisco, expecting Mother to call off her bluff. Instead, she called mine. There I was, boarding a plane to San Francisco just to keep from losing face. Pride is a terrible thing.

The plane trip lasted for what seemed like years but was only hours. I thought about a lot of things: that I wouldn't see my friends for at least three months and that I wouldn't see my great-grandmother or Mom for a long time. I was giving up what at that moment seemed to be everything just to see the man who was my blood father – a man whose face I couldn't even remember. I fell asleep feeling upset and wondering what would happen to me. I awoke when the plane landed.

I quietly picked up my briefcase full of Mr. Marvel comic books, while listening to the stewardess over the speaker welcoming us to San Francisco. I got off the plane, and thought that through the crowd ahead I could see the man who could be no one else except my father. The resemblance between us was amazing. We started to walk toward each other, and when we met it seemed to be an explosion of love. We shook hands and he expressed how happy he was to see me and took my briefcase. Then he introduced me to a strange woman, Jerry, whom I supposed was my stepmother. We went and picked up my luggage and went to the car.

▼

One day, Dad, Jerry, and I were invited over to a friend of Dad's for dinner. She appeared to be quite a nice lady, though I thought she was quite tall for a woman; not at all what I was used to. She kept having me run down to the corner store for odds and ends. On the last run she bent over to get some money out of her purse. Quite by accident, I happened to glance down the front of her dress. There on her chest was all this hair. Realizing that she was a he about caused me to go into a coma. It was the last thing I expected. Maybe all those things Mom had said about Dad were true!

Then, about a week later, they had a friend of theirs from work come over to style my hair. His name was Claude. I had met him once before and could tell he was gay. As he was cutting my hair, his crotch kept pushing itself into my shoulder. It was definitely a turn-on, and at that moment I came to the conclusion that I could be nothing but gay. Claude, wherever you are, thank you for that meaningful shove that helped me make up my mind as to who I was and am.

▼

I recall that I used to put on my tight white jeans and go walking down Polk Street, which was widely known as a gay street. I would walk the whole street and come back again looking and hoping someone would notice me and pick me up, but I never had any luck except for once a man asked me if he could walk with me. I answered with a polite "no" and went on my way home, later wondering why and regretting it.

▼

Finally, my days of skipping school caught up with me and Dad received a note asking why I had been missing so much school. Well, Dad tried to have a father-son talk; I must give him credit for that. Only he said a few things I didn't quite care for. He said I wasn't going to come between Jerry and him (which I wasn't trying to do anyway), and that running away wouldn't solve anything.

I never would have thought about leaving, but he had gone and planted the idea in my head. That was the night I decided to become a runaway ... a decision that wasn't so smart, but I'll never regret it, no, never. The next night I kept arguing with myself whether to do it or not. Finally, I took thirty-six dollars from the desk, hung my keys on the door, and then, with only the clothes on my back and a bag containing my drawings, I walked out the door, which locked behind me. For me, there was no turning back.

It was the first time I had ever been out at night, except for the night I went to the house of Reverend Moon's church and ate dinner there. I walked to the Greyhound bus station, and I purchased a bus ticket for Los Angeles. I picked Los Angeles on pure instinct, and because it was the only place I could go on the money I had.

I boarded the bus at ten-thirty on a Sunday night and it left at eleven. By this time Dad and Jerry would have discovered that I had left. As I recall, at the second stop after we had left San Francisco, an old man got on and sat down beside me. I was listening to the two guys sitting behind me when he struck up a conversation. He asked me where I was heading and I told him. Then he asked me how old I was and I lied and said I was eighteen. Then we just talked about life ... his ending and mine beginning. About an hour before we would hit L.A., he got off the bus. I remember saying to him that I didn't know what would happen to me and he said in an all-knowing voice, "You'll be fine. You're gonna live through a lot of hell, but you'll make it ... Just depend on luck." I watched him get off, and he faded away into a crowd of faces.

I kind of had a feeling that I had just talked to my guardian angel.

We arrived in Los Angeles at six a.m., and I went to the bus station cafeteria and had some coffee while I smoked some cigarettes. I was in no hurry. After all, I had no place to go. Finally, I got up and left. I walked around downtown L.A. for a few hours. Finally, I decided to go to Hollywood. I got the 45 bus and stayed on from one end to the other. By this time, I had gotten more than a bit depressed and had decided to end it all by getting a cheap motel room and slicing my wrists. But then, before I got off the bus, I decided to call my father and have him send for me. I caught a bus back to L.A. and went to the Bonaventure Motel. I got five dollars in change and tried to reach him, but no one answered the phone. I went back outside and wandered around a bit till I came to a church. I went in. It was the most beautiful church I had ever been in. I walked up to the altar and knelt, praying for God to help me.

When I left the church, I returned to the motel. By this time it was about eight o'clock and I was a bit hungry and thirsty, so I went to the underground mall across the street and got a coke and hamburger in a little snack shop. I sat and ate. An adorable busboy came out and started to clean up. When he was through, he came over and sat down beside me. He asked my name, and for a while I showed him my drawings. He really liked one, and I said he could have it if he'd let me sleep on his couch. He agreed, and went to check out, taking the drawing with him. He went through two doors and I never saw him again.

It was ten o'clock when I went back to the motel. I had decided to sleep in the lobby. I plopped myself down on one of the circular couches, but every time I fell asleep, a guard would wake me up and say, "You can sit here as long as you like, but you can't sleep." By this time I was getting more than a bit frustrated, so I got up and left. I'd take my business elsewhere.

I found myself walking the deserted streets of downtown L.A. at four the next morning and decided to go back to the motel. This time I sat by the pool. About six a.m., I went back inside looking for a coffee shop that might be open.

I was walking through a hallway when this gorgeous black security guard came toward me. I said to myself, "David, you're in trouble now," but to my surprise, he asked if he could help me. We ended up in a deep conversation. Finally, he asked if I was gay and I said yes. It seems that he was, too.

His name was Jade, and he told me that he lived with his lover, Fred, and they managed an apartment. He said that if I needed a place to stay I could stay with them, and I accepted.

We arrived at his apartment at nine on a Tuesday morning early in March. As I recall, Fred was asleep on the couch. Jade asked me if I'd like to see some of the vacant apartments. I, being the naïve child, said yes.

He led me into the first one, which hadn't any furniture, and I didn't think it was worth looking at. The second one had a couch, but it hadn't been cleaned yet. He then took me into the walk-in closet and started kissing me. My natural desire for sex was of course taking control of me, but because of my upbringing, I felt it wasn't the right time or place. So I found the words and managed to get myself out of a tight spot. Then we went back to their apartment, and I went into their bedroom and fell into a very deep sleep.

▼

I finally told Jade my true age, and he took me to the Gay Community Center in Hollywood. We talked to a lawyer to see what could be done to ensure that no one tried to cart me off somewhere I didn't want to go.

We found out that as long as I didn't break any laws I couldn't be touched. Then I was told about a youth rap every Friday night at eight where I could meet people my own age. I wasn't too thrilled about this, because kids had always made fun of me because of the way I talk.

While waiting to catch the bus, Jade told me I would have to be careful every time I came to Hollywood, for there were pimps who would grab you off the streets, take you home, and rape you, and then have you work the streets for them with no hope of getting away. It painted a very ugly picture in my mind, and I promised to be very careful always. Then I cheerfully added, "After all, if I was going to work the streets, I would certainly want my own boss – me!"

The first Friday night after that I didn't go, but throughout the following week, Jade and Fred kept saying I should, so I went. I had bought a pair of tight blue jeans and a new shirt the day before, so I wore them, and Jade gave me five dollars and told me to get something to eat, and if it was late to catch a cab back. He said if I rode the bus back after eleven p.m. I might get picked up for prostitution. As I walked out the door, I casually said I'd bring me back a man.

I boarded the bus and was there by seven. There was a Jack-in-the-Box right next door, so I went in and got something to eat. I took my tray and grabbed a window seat so that I could cruise the guys as they walked by. I felt great. I was on my own, or so I thought...

I was sitting there silently sipping my coke and smoking a cigarette when two beautiful guys walked by. One was kind of short with blondish, long hair. The other was tall, blond, and had a good tan. He was wearing ever-so-tight blue jeans, a tight silk shirt, a leather vest, a studded belt, and had a leather key strap attached to his belt loop. I fell in love. I wished later it had been lust.

I immediately dumped my tray and walked out. I followed this couple right into the Center. Once inside, I saw them talking to a girl. I went up and asked if this was the right place for the youth rap. She said yes and introduced herself, and then introduced me to the short guy, whose name was Bobby, and then to Ray, who reached out and shook my hand. I felt electricity surge through my whole body, and then he and Bobby wandered away and started to talk to someone else. For once in my life, I wanted somebody so badly that I decided to reach out and grab him while I still had the chance.

When the youth rap was to begin, we all entered a room rimmed with couches. Bobby and Ray sat down, and I sat down where the next couch began, with only the arms of the two couches between us. The rap session began and so did I — on my deliciously evil plan on how to get this hunk for my own purposes. I just didn't know what had gotten into me. I guess it was love...

I withdrew a cigarette, and before I could get my matches out, Ray had lit it, and then he lit one of his own. Bobby just smiled, and his eyes told me what he was thinking: "Kid, you don't have a chance."

I started chain-smoking, and Ray kept lighting them as fast as I could get them out. Finally, he ran out, and I let him smoke mine. When we stopped for a break, both of us had run out of cigarettes. He went out and brought back two packs. He gave me one and I tried to give him money for it, but he refused. Again, I looked into Bobby's eyes and read his thoughts: "But, then again, maybe you do have a chance, kid."

For another hour, Ray lit my cigs, till the meeting came to an end. He and Bobby were getting ready to leave when I asked Ray if he had a car. He said yes, and I said I needed a lift home and could give him a couple of dollars for gas. He said okay, and we loaded up into a '72 Vega.

Bobby and I were talking about transvestites, until the conversation was suddenly called to a halt as we pulled up to the gas station. Then, when we pulled out, Ray started talking to Bobby about leaving Job Corps and moving into Bobby's place. Bobby didn't like this idea at all, because, as he put it, he didn't want to be tied down to anyone.

▼

We went to my place and went in, and this time Fred was home. I asked him if Ray could stay the night; he said yes and then went into the bedroom. He came back with sheets and a small tube of KY stuck inside a towel. He also handed me the keys to a vacant apartment.

I took Ray up to the room and we talked for a couple of hours, hours that seemed forever to me, who felt like a bride on her wedding night waiting for her new husband to get out of the john and into the bed. As we talked, I started to get excited sexually. Ray slipped his hand over onto my lap, then he gave me a look of genuine surprise. He then apologized for not being "well hung." My lord, when I finally got his clothes off, I discovered he was hung like a Greek god, and he looked like one in every other aspect also. Needless to say, the rest of the night passed with neither of us getting any sleep at all. I was in love...

Joanne, 18

York, Pennsylvania

When I remember being a lesbian in high school, I think of feeling alone, sneaking around feeling hunted, and fighting with my parents. I didn't think that my parents or my friends would understand me, so I kept my secret well. If I hadn't known other lesbians, my life would have been unbearable. On the other hand, if it hadn't been for them, my home life would have run much more smoothly.

▼

I came out to myself as a fourteen-year-old high school sopho-more. My field hockey teammates had been spreading a rumor that our coach was a lesbian. I was angry that they would let such a thing influence their opinion of her. I didn't think I'd ever met any gays, and I knew nothing about homosexuality. Nonetheless, from my uneducated standpoint, I decided that their attitudes were unjust.

The constant talk about gays made me curious. I went to the library to read up on the subject. I told myself that this was so I could better understand my coach if indeed she was gay.

But one day, a short time after I starting to read about lesbians, I was sitting in English class and with a flash like a bolt of lightning, I realized that I was gay. The "bolt of lightning" line may sound rather dramatic, but suddenly all the feelings of attraction I had been having for women, along with my feelings of isolation due to my lack of "femininity," came together. And they pointed to the label "lesbian." I walked around like a shell-shock victim for days. I don't remember the exact thoughts that ran through my head at the time, but along with the fear of being a social outcast came a slight pleasure. I had always prided myself on being different, and this was certainly keeping to my pattern.

I knew I had to find someone to talk to. My first instinct was to approach my hockey coach. I imagined telling her of my feelings and her immediately confessing that she was also a lesbian. We would then fall into each other's arms and comfort each other, sharing the loneliness faced by deviants in a hostile world.

Needless to say, this did not happen. Quite the opposite. She told me I was just nervous around boys and should make an attempt to be around them more. I was crushed. That was definitely not what I wanted to hear. Nonetheless, I decided to do as she said, because at that point I thought I was the only lesbian on earth. Soon after deciding to "go straight," I got a boyfriend and went out with him three times. But I quickly realized the futility of denying my attraction to women and abruptly stopped seeing him. I felt that no matter how much I felt for a man, I would always be drawn most to women.

It was in October that I realized my lesbianism, and not until the next April that I finally found someone gay to talk with. Looking back over my journal entries from that time period, I recall the anguish I suffered. I wrote several things along these lines:

Please. Help me. Oh shit, I have to talk with someone. Help me please. My feelings are turning into gnawing monsters trying to clamber out. Oh please ... I want to just jump out that window and try to kill myself. Maybe I'll get sympathy then. Maybe they'll try to understand ... I have to tell someone, ask someone. WHO??!! Dammit all, would someone please help me? Someone, anyone. Help me. I'm going to kill myself if they don't.

Finally, in April, I heard about a women's softball team that was reputed to have lesbians on it. I joined as soon as I could, hoping that the rumors were true. While playing, I dropped as many hints as I could to let the team know I was gay. I thought I was being subtle, but looking back, I think I must have been pretty obvious. My lack of discretion paid off, though, because finally one team member felt comfortable enough to come out to me. We talked for a long time that night. We became friends, and I began to rely on her for a great deal of support. She became my mentor for that whole summer.

▼

Everything would have been perfect except for my parents.

I had finally found people to talk with, because my first gay friend introduced me to other lesbians. All were at least eighteen, and most were over twenty-one. At first, my parents merely thought it odd that I would be hanging around older people so much or, rather, that they would hang around me. Then my home life fell apart when someone told my mother that my softball coach was gay.

She automatically assumed that the rest of the team was also gay and forbade me to socialize with team members. She would not let me go on tournaments overnight either, for fear of what would happen in a dark room full of lesbians.

Eventually, at the beginning of my junior year, I had my first lover. She was nineteen, and my parents suspected the truth about our relationship, so they forbade me to socialize with anyone out of high school. Since I knew no lesbians in school, the restriction was extremely unpleasant. Obviously, the limitations included my lover, so I had to do a lot of sneaking around in order to see her. That was when most of the lying started. I would say I was going out with my friends from school and instead would meet her somewhere. At night, after my parents had gone to bed, she would throw stones at my second-floor window and I would slip down the back stairs of our house to meet her. Every creak on the floor sounded like a gunshot, and as I snuck out, the dog would bark, because I did not let her out with me. I still cannot believe my parents never heard all the commotion. After playing Romeo and Juliet for about two months, my lover understandably got tired of sneaking about like a hunted fox and broke off the relationship. It was painful to end, but it was also a relief not to be lying to my parents so much.

▼

Following the breakup of my romance, I decided I had had enough of family fights and resolved to be a perfect daughter. As an athlete, I refused to smoke or drink anyway, but at that point, my resolve gained a second significance. I determined that when my parents found out I was gay, they would not be able to kick me out of the house, because I would be a model daughter in every other way. I stopped picking on my younger siblings, started to work hard in school, and generally did whatever my parents told me to do. They started to trust me again, and I found myself once again in their favor. I made a point to develop friendships with people my own age and talked about boys as much as possible. I even started wearing skirts and dresses more frequently. One benefit of this frenzied perfectionism was an improved grade point average, which allowed me to go to the college I wanted to.

I wish to emphasize that although my having older gay friends served to complicate my life, I would have been a mental wreck without them. The women I knew let me know in no uncertain terms that I was not abnormal: that my sexuality was healthy and normal. Despite this general encouragement, though, they also often urged me to lead a heterosexual life, at least until I got out of high school. Few of them had been gay as early as I was, but they could easily foresee the difficulties I would face. Another reason they discouraged my lesbianism was that I was under eighteen. That meant no one would have a relationship with me for fear of being discovered and arrested for seducing a minor. On that, they were right. Except for my one lover in eleventh grade, no one else in my area did approach me as more than a friend until I graduated from high school.

Despite my friends' advice, I chose to continue calling myself a lesbian and refused to play heterosexual games. There were difficult problems involved, but to establish one identity and stick with it helped me. Fortunately, my friends were supportive, for the most part. Nonetheless, the mixed advice was often confusing. This confusion led me to write the following poem, one of several I composed during this time:

> I have a problem, I feel so sad.
> I'm going crazy, it's getting bad.
> The friends I have that aren't like me
> tell me I am wrong.
> The ones I know who really are
> tell me I'm too young.
> How am I wrong when it's in my heart?
> Am I too young when I fit the part?

I am gay, that I know,
but to my friends that is not so.
How to cope with folk like these?
Are they or I the ones I please?

The words of my friends often encouraged me, but their lives gave me more strength. I saw their relationships with other women, and for the most part, those bonds of intimacy let me see that there could be happiness in my life. I saw that these women were not the fat, ugly, man-hating butches that were so often portrayed in stereotypes. I found that I could be just like everyone else in my society and still have intimate relationships with women.

I succeeded in my efforts to be as perfect a daughter as I could be, but I also managed to be brainwashed in the process. I did not realize what a pile of mush my brain had become until this year, in my second semester of college. My parents found out that I was a lesbian and sent me to a psychologist to be "cured." I am presently being cured, not of my sexual orientation, but of the way I accepted my parents' every word as gospel. In my attempt to be perfect, arguing with them was not part of the program. The easiest solution to disagreements was essentially to agree with them. My parents are conservative, upper-middle-class Roman Catholics, and their morals and demands reflect that background. With those kinds of values surrounding me, it was easier to accept their standards than to defend my lifestyle against them.

It has been five months since I admitted my homosexuality to my parents. Even though they both say they still love me, they still hope that I will one day let go of my feelings for women. I have assured them that I do not hate men and would not pass up a heterosexual relationship on the basis of my lover's sex, yet they continue to be disappointed in my decision.

The worst part is that my parents blame my older friends for influencing me. They feel that seeing older lesbians who were like "normal" people made me think it was acceptable for myself as well. Yes, these friends did help me accept myself, but they did not intentionally influence me to be gay. I was a lesbian for six months before I met anyone to talk to. My friends did not change me; they merely helped me stay sane. I do not know if I am or ever was capable of killing myself, but I sometimes think I might have done so had I been forced into three years of lesbian solitude.

My parents also feel that I was too young to make such a decision in high school. Now I am eighteen and they still think I am too young to decide that I am emotionally, mentally, and physically attracted to women. I am not, nor was I ever, too young to make the decisions I have made. I only hope that other young people like myself can have a support group to suit their emotional needs. I searched all over for any type of group to write to, and when I finally found one, I was too afraid to write, for fear that the organization would not use discretion when returning my mail.

I also hope that an alternative to the bars is developed to meet people's social needs. As a fifteen-year-old trying to sneak into bars where the drinking age is twenty-one, I was not very successful. And when I did get into a bar, I hated it, because it was superficial. On the other hand, it was so nice to be there, because I knew no one there objected to me solely because I was gay, and I could relax with my identity.

What high school lesbians and gays need most is the support of older homosexuals, gay people their own age, and, of course, their parents. I would have been ecstatic to find a support group that recognized the existence of teenage gays ... and mostly just to discover that there were others out there like myself.

Gary Dowd, 20

Irvine, California

Life is full of little ironies. My particular favorite at this moment concerns my parents. My parents keep telling me that life will be horrible as a gay person, since I will be constantly badgered by society. The irony is that they do more badgering than anyone else – though to be honest, the situation is not as bad as it may seem; in fact, it's pretty good. Overall, my coming out was well received. This was due partially to planning, and partially (I'm embarrassed to admit) to luck.

Despite my occasional sloppiness, I was never "discovered" before I came out, so I was lucky in being able to come out when I wanted to. A friend of mine did not have this luxury, and it made life pretty tough for him. His parents started screening his phone calls, wouldn't let him go out, and made him go to a psychiatrist, among other things. As time went on, things improved, but it serves as a reminder of how dangerous the situation can be if coming out is not done carefully.

Before I came out, the idea kept running through my head that once you come out, you're out for good. Yes, people might pretend that you never came out, even *you* might pretend that you never did, but if everyone pretended that the sky wasn't blue, it wouldn't change the color. Keeping this in mind, I knew that when I came out I had to do it well, so I started my research.

I didn't exactly go around with a clipboard taking notes and later write myself a report, but instead, I just kept the idea of research in my mind, and thought about how I could be prepared. I found that talking with other gays and lesbians was the most helpful. It was encouraging to hear the successful stories, but it also was discouraging to hear about the failures. I collected a lot of information about what is generally good and bad to do, and also had the pleasure of some great conversations. I tried to talk with a wide range of people to get different perspectives, so I sometimes had to force myself to talk to complete strangers. Of course, this was also a great excuse to meet people.

I also found some good information in books, but had some difficulties with libraries. I did not find many books on homosexuality, and those few did not have much information that was applicable. I was also reluctant at the time to walk up to the checkout counter with gay books, so I often hid in dark corners to read them. In the long run, the most helpful books I found were those that I borrowed from friends, and gay and lesbian organizations.

The most important thing for me about coming out was knowing that I was ready to do it. Before I came out to anyone, I wanted to feel one hundred percent comfortable and content with my gayness, and experienced enough to know what I was talking about. From talking with other gays and lesbians, I learned that I would probably need to do a lot of defending and explaining, so I planned on being prepared. This was something very important that I was doing for myself, and I wanted to do the best job possible. It was only when I reached that point that I felt I was ready to come out.

The first people I came out to were close friends. That seemed to be the safest place to start, since I felt that a truly good friend would not let it get in the way of the friendship. However, it was still scary as all hell. I was about as paranoid as I've ever been, imagining all sorts of horrible results, but as it turned out, things worked out very well and there was no real change in any of the friendships. Sometimes, good friends turn out to be not so good. I consider myself lucky, since all my close friends were understanding and dealt with the subject maturely.

Telling the first person was the hardest, since I had no idea what it was going to be like. I had decided that I was going to tell my three best friends, and I decided on the order I was going to do it in and then set a "due date" for myself. I ended up haunting myself with the due date for about two weeks before I finally told the first friend. I kept waiting for the perfect moment, but there was always something wrong. Eventually, I realized that the perfect moment was not going to come, so I settled for a reasonably good one. Finally, I pushed myself to say, "Guess what, I'm gay!" Somehow, I got away with it. We talked about being gay and then about life in general, and everything went smoothly. When it was all over, I felt amazingly good about myself for forcing myself to do it — it was well worth it. After that, telling became easier and easier with each person, until it was time to tell my parents.

I knew that telling my parents would not be easy. If everything goes wrong when you tell a friend, you can always just walk away from it, but with your parents you're risking a lot more and it becomes a great deal harder. Even though I know my parents well, I still wasn't sure how they would react. From my experience with coming out to friends, I knew that anything can happen, and with parents this is even more true because of their being your parents and also because of the age difference. I knew that I needed to be prepared for anything, since their response could range from complete hysterics to casual acceptance to even happiness. It was not easy being prepared for such a range, but when I finally felt like I could handle the situation, a battleship could have fallen from the sky and I would have known what to do.

As well as I could, I set the situation to my advantage. I made sure that I had hours, if necessary, to talk it over, and I also made sure that my father or mother and I would be alone, so they could be honest and comfortable and not have to worry about an audience.

Things went smoother than I expected. I had expected hysterics from my mother and worse from my father, but both responded calmly. They asked quite a few questions, and at times tried to describe my "dark future" (based on their knowledge of stereotypes and limited personal experience), but overall they were very understanding. Their calm reaction seemed to result mostly from my calmness in telling them. Had I told them during a fight or in some other negative way, it more than likely would have resulted in a bad response.

Once I passed the difficult part of saying, "I'm gay," it became fun and at times funny. Hearing things like "What did I do that made you gay?" or "Are you sure you're gay?" made it very difficult not to laugh, since it pointed out just how little my parents really knew about the subject. It seemed very ironic to me that I had all the experience and they were asking all the questions. However, this irony also presented a problem. Parents are used to having all the experience and knowledge, so it is difficult for them to believe that you really know what you are doing. Sometimes it took a lot of patience on my part to deal with the frustration and keep things running smoothly.

My parents always surprise me whenever the subject of homosexuality comes up. Sometimes it's a good surprise, sometimes not so good. There have been times when I've sat with them and talked positively about my gayness for hours, and there are times when they refuse to talk about it at all. I've noticed that over a period of time their attitude goes in and out (of the closet) like waves on the beach. I keep wishing that they will adjust overnight, which is ridiculous considering how long it took *me* to adjust. But they are progressing, and I find that encouraging.

Probably the most annoying aspect of my parents' attitude is that they keep hoping that I will become straight, despite my telling them that the chances of that are about the same as the chances of them becoming gay. I think I would have to be a saint to always be patient when I hear them say something about "growing out of it" or "not meeting the right girl," but I have learned that they are doing it only because they are concerned and love me. They can't completely believe that I can be happy and gay (sorry about the pun) at the same time, so they hope I'll go straight so I "can have a happy life." I can only be patient, remind them that I *am* happy, and continue to guide them in the right direction.

In retrospect, I'm very glad that I came out to both my friends and my family. There have been difficulties, and it was definitely a risk, but the resulting rewards and freedom made it worth all the planning and waiting. Now my life is in the world, and only my clothes are in the closet.

Aimee Anderson, 17

Ft. Lauderdale, Florida

My mom is a lesbian. I live with her and her lover Bonnie. We consider ourselves a family. We *are* a family. We have our troubles, but we manage. We live in the Mermaid Inn. It's a lesbian motel that my mom owns.

I'm seventeen years old. My mom came out to me when I was twelve. I wasn't exactly thrilled with her new lifestyle. And Bonnie seemed to come into my mom's life so quickly. I was not used to seeing my mom in love. Most of all, I felt left out.

All these dykes started coming over. I pretended I didn't want anything to do with them. But the truth was, I wanted to be friends with them. Soon I began to look to them for guidance and support, even though I thought I was straight.

At fourteen, though, there came a turning point. I fell in love with a woman! A 39-year-old woman! Nothing came of the infatuation beyond a very special friendship. I still look to this woman for support; I think she gave me the strength I needed to search for my own identity. That same year, we moved from Gainesville to Ft. Lauderdale. I remember being brokenhearted. I had to leave my unrequited love behind.

During my first year in Ft. Lauderdale, I lived the life of an average teenage girl – except I didn't date boys. I had crushes, but they were always on girls. I came out when I was fifteen.

I started going to a gay youth group at the MCC church. I found an incredible amount of support there. I also met two young lesbians at the group who went to my high school. They were lovers. I had suspected that they might be. There were rumors flying all over the school about them. There were rumors about me, too. When the three of us started hanging out, the other kids really started talking. That whole year was hard.

Recently, those two women dropped out of school. So now I'm left alone to battle the ignorance of teenagers and stubborn authority figures. So far, though, my junior year doesn't seem as hard.

Even though I know a lot of lesbians here in Ft. Lauderdale, I haven't met many who are my own age. And the ones I have met have been very insecure about being gay. They are not comfortable with themselves yet. There aren't very many places gay kids can go to hang out.

Older women don't take me very seriously – even at the Mermaid Inn, my own home! One time a woman said in a very degrading way, "How old are you? You can't be more than twelve!" I was offended. There are also women who wonder if I'll always be a lesbian. I think it's because I'm young and because my mom's a lesbian.

Right now, I just try to do my best. I am out at school, and I've marched in the gay and lesbian pride march. I feel like the more visible I am, the less scary it might feel to some kid in school who is struggling with her sexuality (or his). I like to think of myself as an aspiring activist.

Michael, 16

Georgia

Growing up was strange. When I'd go fishing with my friends, I was always more interested in watching them than I was in the fish! When I got to junior high, I was in heaven. I found myself watching boys in gym and in the locker room. Why was I feeling this way? Why?

This went on for three years. I couldn't handle the names I was called. I couldn't handle the fact that I was a "homo boy," a "faggot," a "dick-sucker," and a "queer." I wanted out. I tried to kill myself. I was in a mental hospital for four months.

After I got out, I joined a support group for young gays. Now I can say I'm gay. So what if I am? If someone has a problem with it, they should go deal with it. I've come out to almost all of my friends. Sometimes it was hell, but nothing compares to holding it inside. My parents know too. My father disowned me. My stepfather tells me it will change. My mother is cool with it.

I'd like to say to other gay teens that I hope your coming out will be as easy as possible for you. Being gay is not the end of the world. Be strong. I don't want anyone to end up dead like I almost did. Thank God I didn't.

Kimba Hunter, 18

Alberta, Canada

I had a label for my feelings when I was thirteen, but it wasn't until I was sixteen that I came out. First, I told a male friend of mine. I really don't remember how the subject came up. I was in an institution with him at the time. After we got out, we lost contact for a time. When we got back in touch, we started to talk about being gay. He was gay too. I finally got to a point where I said I would go to GATE (Gay Alliance Towards Equality).

Several times, I turned around and wasn't going to go through with it. I was terrified! I didn't know what to expect. The most I knew about being gay was from when my mom had spoken of a couple of gay women she knew, and I got to thinking of them as women dressed like tough men who would beat you up if you looked at them the wrong way.

When I finally got to GATE, I stood outside the door for ten or fifteen minutes, ready to run. Once I got in there, I studied the other people. It's a Friday I will never forget. The men didn't look like escapees from a dancing school, and the women were friendly. These were normal people! Maybe I belonged here after all. The next time I went, a woman counselor took me into the office and explained what GATE was. She asked me how I knew that I was gay and a few other questions.

Soon after that, I started going regularly to GATE, and I had to ask my group home parents if I could stay out until eleven. They asked why, but I refused to tell them. A couple of days later, I was on the phone to my friend and I told him that they wanted to know where I was going so much. He was afraid they were going to give me a hassle. But he said he would tell them where I had been going. So when one of them came into the kitchen where the phone was, I asked if she wanted to know where I had been going. She said yes, so shaking like crazy, I told her, "GATE." She asked what GATE was and I handed her the phone. She asked my friend, but all he told her was that it was a break in a fence that swung open so you could get to the other side. She did eventually find out what GATE was. I was lucky, because for the next three months that they were my house parents, she and her husband gave me acceptance and support.

After I had been going to GATE for a while, I started to come out to other people as well. I got letters from friends I'd written to, saying that I would never truly be happy with a woman; that being gay was wrong and bad. It was hard getting this reaction to my happiness at finding others like me and at understanding myself better. I had been warned but didn't really understand how much it could hurt.

I had been out for four months when my grandmother on my dad's side of the family died. I went down south to be with my dad. My cousin came up for the funeral. I had told her I was gay, trying to share my happiness and hoping she would understand. She didn't. Sitting in my dad's car, we finally had a chance to talk. She sat on one side and I was on the other. She refused to hug me and said she didn't want to touch me anymore, for fear of turning me on. I pointed out that she was my cousin, but it didn't matter. I felt hurt and angry. What had I done to deserve this? More than a year later, she still refuses to even write. I have come to terms with it now. It wasn't easy.

My younger brother also wasn't going to talk to me anymore because of it. We got in a few arguments and talked some. Now, we get along again. I knew that he had accepted me when he gave me one of his magazines of naked women. My younger sister accepted it, and we have had some good talks.

With my mom, I know it was hard for her to accept. She still says I am running from reality, but she leaves me alone. She went through what I call her "grandmother" stage. Every time we passed babies' things or baby products, she'd say something about grandchildren and look at me meaningfully. That was hard to handle. I know she wants lots of grandchildren, but I won't be giving her any. The subject still comes up, but it isn't constant now.

My dad wanted me to fight it. I told him I had tried. I didn't go through a homosexual stage; I went through a heterosexual stage, trying to figure out what was so great about guys sexually. I still don't understand. I guess that, for straights, it's like it is for me when I am with a woman. I also told my dad I wasn't happy when I tried that. I experimented in whatever ways I thought would make a difference, but it was no go. My closest friends are guys; there is caring and closeness between us.

When other people find out that I am gay, I have found some accept it and are curious about it. I try to answer their questions as openly and nondefensively as I can. I figure that if they accept me and are willing to try and understand, then I can try to help them understand. I think a lot of the prejudice against gays comes from a lack of understanding.

While I was in the group home, my first three months after coming out were filled with acceptance and support. My next three months were hell! The group home became staffed. I resented the staff, because I felt that they were responsible for the group home parents' leaving, even though I knew it to be untrue. On top of my being upset at that, two of the staff members wanted to "help" me. One was going to Bible school to be a minister; the other was an avid Christian. I was told that two thousand years ago, I would have been stoned to death. That shook me up a little. At the time, I had next to no understanding of the Bible, nor did I want any. They quoted the Bible to me, told me I would never have true sexual satisfaction, and asked me if I didn't want a man's strong arms around me. I didn't really care if I went to Hell or not; if I had cared, I would have really been in bad shape. But in response to all these Bible quotes, more than a few times I stomped down to GATE ... mainly out of frustration at being unable to defend myself with other Bible quotes or some other defense on their level so that I'd be left alone. At GATE I found understanding and caring. I still felt miserable, but GATE helped a lot. Without the understanding and caring and support of the many staff people I met at GATE, I don't think I could have made it. A lot of times I wanted to give up, but with their help, I found the strength to go on.

After three months, one of the group home staff people I was having trouble with talked to me. From that time we have been friends. Believe it or not, after all that hassle, we are very close and have a deep understanding and trust.

There are some prison inmates that I am writing to who have all helped me in one way or another — by helping me to get a thicker skin or by giving encouragement and understanding. Two are straight but accept me as I am. Another one is straight and thinks I should grow up and face reality. (Gays are against God, hate their parents, and are responsible for all the miserable things in life.) When I read that letter, I ripped it in half. Things like that are responsible for all the bad in the world.

The other two prisoners I write to are gay and very supportive. Through writing to them, I have become more positive, accept myself a lot more, and have discovered that I am okay. I have gotten close to them, and they have also helped me to be more understanding, so I don't get mad or hurt so easily when the subject of homosexuality comes up in a negative context.

I hope that I can somehow help others understand gays better, and make it easier for others to come out and think more positively about themselves, because they are special people too.

Sue Cline, 17
Diane Rodriguez, 18

Chicago, Illinois

Sue: I'm a senior at St. Scholastica High School in Chicago. I'm seventeen years old, and I am gay. Being gay is something I never really thought about until I was thirteen. All along I had had feelings for women, but I never really put a name to it.

I was thirteen and a freshman when I met my first lover, Carla. Before we were lovers, we were really close friends. After a few months, the relationship began to get physical. It was about then that I started thinking seriously about being gay. It wasn't until my sophomore year that I finally decided for sure that I was gay.

Both my parents and my classmates expected me to date. I had a few boyfriends who were straight, but I knew one or two gay guys and we covered for each other.

Being gay at an all-girls Catholic school is really hard. It is even harder when your lover goes to school with you, and you can't do anything, because the slightest sign of affection labels you for four years of school. At first, only one of our friends knew we were lovers. She took it really well and, unlike some of our other friends, always stood by us. Because Carla and I were so close, many people at school immediately guessed. That was really hard, because people can be cruel when they don't understand. Some people just didn't talk to us. It got easier after Carla and I broke up in our junior year, because then I started dating people outside of school.

I am a senior now, in the midst of a wonderful relationship with another girl that I met at school. We both love each other, but it took us a long time to get where we are now. When I first met her, I practically fell head over heels in love with her. She didn't really seem to care much about anything, even her friends, so I decided to get to know her.

My relationship with Carla was almost over, because she had met a boy. Diane and I got really close, even though our friends did not approve. She felt guilty about Carla, though, and it wasn't until just before she graduated that I told her that I loved her. When she hugged me and told me that she loved me too, it was the happiest moment of my life. Since then, we've really gotten to know each other, and we're now planning to spend the rest of our lives together.

Neither of our families know about us, but someday we hope to move in together and tell them. A lot of our friends know; they accept us for what we are, and don't hassle us. I love being with her, and I like watching her. She has taught me a great deal about myself. I used to be so sick of my life and my world, but now she has changed my whole outlook on life. To me, being with her makes every day worth living and special. I love her in a very special way, one I've never felt before. It's wonderful to be gay!

Being gay was always something I just accepted. I never felt guilty about it, and never would have hidden it if not for pressure from society. When I was a sophomore, I wandered into a gay youth group called Horizons, where I got to meet a lot of people my age who knew just where I was coming from. Later, after I stopped going to Horizons, I joined the Metropolitan Community Church (MCC), which is nondenominational and mostly gay. MCC did a lot of good for me, because I met slightly older people, eighteen and up, who were out on their own. Since I turned sixteen, I've become very open, telling a few more close friends.

Probably my favorite part of being gay is being open enough to tell my friends, and to walk out in public with Diane holding hands or kissing. I've become involved in several lesbian and women's groups and coffeehouses, and have grown a lot from them. Most of the people I've told knew already – but it isn't until they see Diane and me together that it really hits them. Thankfully, most of my close friends took it well enough that I didn't lose them.

I haven't told my parents that I'm gay yet, and probably won't for quite a while either. I don't think they would understand. In fact, I should say that I know they wouldn't. They knew about Carla and me, and they thoroughly disapproved. So until I'm of age, I won't tell them.

I guess what I'd like to say most to the people who read this book is that if you're gay, be proud of yourself, because it isn't wrong or bad. Also, try and find a way to contact the gay community through youth groups, community centers, bookstores, or newspapers.

▼

Diane: When I was little, I always thought I would get married, have children, and stay home cooking, cleaning, and doing all the things housewives do. I expected such a future until I turned fifteen and started dating. I began to see that there were other things to do. I also began to notice homosexual couples and how happy they seemed. I really envied them and wondered why people didn't like them.

I went to a Catholic high school where they actually said being a homosexual was a terrible sin. I had always been told that it was wrong and dirty, and that homosexuals were perverted and disgusting. I never believed it was wrong or dirty, but I had never thought I might be gay. All I knew was that I envied them and wished I could be as sure of myself as they seemed to be of themselves.

When I was sixteen, I met a boy named Peter, who became my boyfriend soon after we met. I had had a few boyfriends before, none of whom lasted more than two months. I broke up with them because I wasn't happy and I was looking for someone better than the last. I thought Peter was the one. Suddenly I had more friends, because I had such a good-looking boyfriend. Everyone liked him, and I was invited to a lot of parties. I thought I had found what was missing in my life. But after a few months, I began to feel uncomfortable around him. I cringed whenever he touched me. He pushed me too far, and I lost my self-respect, self-confidence, and self-esteem. I broke up with him and withdrew into myself and became very depressed.

I did a lot of serious thinking about my feelings and my life. I knew I didn't want any more boyfriends and that I felt more comfortable around girls. I didn't go out looking for anyone. I just decided to wait and see who I'd meet and let things happen. After having decided that having a relationship with a woman was what I wanted, I felt much better and I didn't feel it was wrong. Society's preaching couldn't change my mind or make me feel bad about it.

A few months later, I met Sue. I fell in love with her and felt wonderful. I had never felt that way about a boy. I am eighteen now, and it has been over a year since I met her and almost a year that we've been lovers. I have never been happier and I have finally found what I had been missing. Sue has helped me regain my self-respect. We have never once thought we are immoral or sinful. I often wonder how people can say it is wrong if they have never tried it.

Being in love is hard to hide, so I decided to tell two of my good friends. We had been friends for four years, and I didn't think it would make a big difference in our friendship. At first, they weren't upset and accepted it. After a couple of weeks, they said we couldn't be friends anymore, because they didn't like Sue, they thought it was wrong, and they absolutely would not accept it. I was very hurt and afraid to tell anyone else, for fear of losing more friends. Then I realized that if my friends couldn't accept me, they weren't worth having as friends. I feel good about myself and that's all that matters to me.

At first I was a little uncomfortable holding Sue's hand in public or having her arm around me even in gay neighborhoods. Now I feel more comfortable. Even though more people are coming out of the closet, some people are still shocked when they see us. A lot of people were surprised when I told them I was gay, because I don't "look like a lesbian." They don't believe I am gay, just because I don't fit the stereotype.

When I first came out, I didn't know many gay people. Sue and I went to Gay Horizons Youth Group, where we met people our age. Since then I have met many people, some younger, some older. I like most of the people I have met, but there are a few I don't like at all. Sue introduced me to two older women who I thought were examples of the butch lesbian stereotype. All they were interested in was how fast and how young they could get girls into bed. We went to a lesbian bar a couple of times. The general impression I got was that most older lesbians were only interested in sex. I honestly do not like the bars and the women in them.

Two months ago I started working at a graphic design firm owned by two women. They are lovers and are very serious about their work. They are sweet and very nice and totally different from the impression I had of older lesbians. I am sure a lot of straight people have the same impression I had, which only makes them misunderstand and dislike gay people even more. They should be made aware that we do not all fit the stereotypes.

I didn't expect a lot of straight people to accept me, but I was really surprised when I realized some of Sue's gay friends didn't accept me. They hardly believe we are still together a year later. They don't believe I am a lesbian, because I have had boyfriends and didn't have a homosexual experience until I was seventeen instead of twelve or fourteen like they did. They think I am using Sue; that this is just a phase I'm going through. At first it really bothered me that they felt this way, but there is nothing I can do to change the way they feel.

Believing in yourself and accepting yourself is very important. No one should feel dirty or immoral or be made to believe it is wrong. No one should ever feel ashamed of something so wonderful. I am proud of who I am, and I love Sue very much. She has taught me a lot about life and helped me through some rough times.

If you love or are attracted to someone, don't deny it, even if you're afraid that you might be gay. Denying it only hurts you. Being gay isn't as terrible as you might think. Once you admit it to yourself, even though it may cause problems with family and friends, you'll be happier and much more comfortable with yourself.

Roy A., 19

San Diego, California

I've always known I was different. I really didn't know in what way, though.

When I was about ten, my friends and I would all play "doctor." There was a field behind my house with tall grass and weeds – a perfect "examining room." While I enjoyed playing with the girls, it was even more fun to play with the boys. I had no idea that this was in any way weird, but none of the other boys in the neighborhood seemed to share my interest in male "patients."

We moved across town in Salt Lake City when I was twelve, and I lost touch with my friends. I became a loner; I didn't have any real friends. I went to school and came home. When I turned sixteen, I went to work at a local pizza restaurant. I fell in love with many of the crew there over the months that followed, but I didn't do anything about it. I was afraid of being fired, or worse. I just went on being lonely.

Then, the summer I was seventeen, something happened that changed my life. I was visiting my dad in Southern California. (He and my mom got a divorce when I was five.) We were out having dinner and he suddenly asked me, "Do you know why your mother and I separated?"

It seemed like a pretty heavy question for the time and place, so I said something like "Because you decided you didn't belong together." There was a long pause like he was about to say something that was really hard for him.

"Do you remember my roommates?"

"Yeah, so?"

"Well, Frank was gay. So was Paul ... and Doug."

"What are you saying?"

"So am I!"

I couldn't believe it. My father had just come out to me. This totally changed my outlook on things. I thought dads were supposed to like moms and have babies with them, not move away and like other guys.

▼

Over the next year, things started falling into place. I realized that I liked guys, not girls. Sure I still had female friends, but not anybody really close. I realized that I couldn't be too strange, because Dad liked them too.

I wrote the Hetrick Martin Institute in New York asking for some information. They sent some articles about AIDS, some comic books called *Tales from the Closet,* and the address of a gay publishing company (this one, in fact). I stayed up all night in my room reading every word. I sent away for a catalog from the publishing company, and over the next six months, I ordered several books. I became a vacuum, gathering every scrap of information I could about this "lifestyle." (I hate that term, "lifestyle." It's not a lifestyle; it's one element of a whole life.) I became more confident in myself. I was not a pervert or a freak. I was that one out of every ten people that is gay.

The next summer, when I went to visit my dad, I came out to him. I got kind of a strange reaction. "It's okay if you really are gay, but I want to see if it's just a phase."

I spent the rest of the summer convincing him that it wasn't just a phase. By the end of the summer, though, I felt comfortable enough around him to point out when I thought someone was cute or had a nice butt.

When I returned home, I came out to my mother. She cried for a week and blamed it on my father. It took me about a month to explain to her that this was just how I was, nobody *made* me this way, and that I sure as hell wouldn't *choose* to be something that most of society (especially in Utah) thought was sick!

I found nothing but dead ends in Utah; I was convinced that there was no gay community there. But I continued with my research. After finding out that my boss was friendly to gays, I dropped a few hints and finally came out to him. His reaction was, "So?"

Well, cool. (I'm certainly not advocating coming out all over the place. Do it only when *you* are ready, and only to people you think you can trust.)

▼

I finally graduated from high school, and ran to California for summer vacation. My dad's friends told me about the gay and lesbian center in San Diego and I found out there was a youth group that met there once a week. So I went. It was the scariest thing I had ever done in my life.

I took a seat and sat there feeling that everyone was staring at me. After what seemed like forever, the leader of the group started the meeting. Everyone took a turn saying their names, how old they were, and whether it was their first time at the meeting.

"My name is Roy. I'm eighteen and this is my first time here." Everyone started clapping. They were applauding me for having the courage to come to the meeting and it felt wonderful!

After the meeting, a bunch of them were going to the beach. I didn't have any way to get there, but I really wanted to go. I was ready to head home, when suddenly I felt a tap on my shoulder. I turned around.

"Are you going to the beach with us?"

"I'd like to, but I don't have a ride."

"Well, you do now."

I followed Torrey and his friends, Lisa and Jonathan, to the parking lot. We drove to the beach and build a bonfire. Torrey sat down next to me and started to talk. We chatted about this and that, and all the while, he was running his fingers through the sand and finding shells, which he dropped into the pocket of my shirt. Why was he doing that? I had no idea, so I just let him keep putting shells in my pocket and talking.

At eleven-thirty or so, we all decided it was time to go home. I climbed back into the car with my pocketful of shells. As we got close to my dad's apartment, Torrey handed me a slip of paper with his phone number on it. And he asked for mine. When the car stopped, he got out to let me out of the backseat. He asked, "Can I have a hug?" I gladly gave him one. This was my first gay hug; Torrey was the first guy I was this close to. It felt so nice, I just let him hold me. Then he got back into the car and drove off.

The next morning he called me, and we wound up spending the rest of the summer together.

Now it's almost a year later, and I'm making the final arrangements to move to California to live with my dad. I did finally find a gay community in Utah, but I find the community in San Diego much friendlier. I have kept in touch with Torrey. He has a lover now, and things will never be the same between us, but I'll always love him.

My advice to someone just coming out would be to gain all the knowledge you can. Like they say, "Knowledge is power."

You got your hands on this book so you must be doing something right! If you have the means, order books through the mail. A good publishing company will send them in a plain package that nobody would suspect. A lot of gay and lesbian organizations have information that they'll send for free. I'm sure that *somewhere* where you live there *is* a gay and lesbian community. You just have to find it. That can be hard to do. Try looking in the yellow pages under "Gay and lesbian." There might be a bookstore in your town with a gay and lesbian section; maybe they'd have more information or a phone number you could call. Some gay and lesbian hotlines have information for almost any city in the country.

The process of coming out to yourself and eventually to others is scary. I know. I've been there. I'm nineteen, and it still scares the heck out of me sometimes. You've gotten this far, and that took guts. You should be proud of yourself. By all means, keep going. Don't even *think* about giving up. The rest of us are rooting for you. Hang in there.

David, 19

Baltimore, Maryland

A ctually, the term "coming out" is more than a bit confusing, because it isn't a single, momentous event, but a series of lengthy stages. Perhaps the most difficult part of this process is realizing and admitting, "I am gay." In my case, there was a gradual awareness that I was different from everyone else. Realizing that I was attracted to my own sex didn't lead to feelings of pride and dignity. My first reactions were very negative, which was to be expected, considering the pervasive stereotypes.

One incident that stands out in my memory occurred when I was around fourteen. My mother and I were watching television when a speaker from a local gay group appeared on one of those half-minute editorial segments that are repeated every so often. After about five seconds, my mother remarked, "I really feel sorry for those people, because they need help. They're really sick!" That just about destroyed the feelings of self-worth I had been working so hard to develop. After a long period of self-hatred, I came to realize that every human being has an inherent beauty. Therefore, some unique beauty existed within me, and I had a contribution to make to the world.

The next step was to admit to someone else what I had discovered about myself. Fortunately, I had a very close friend who virtually dragged it out of me. If it was difficult for me to come to terms with myself, it was nearly as difficult to tell someone else and leave myself open for rejection and harassment. However, when I finally got the nerve to tell my friend that I was gay, the supportive response made all the anxiety in the world worth enduring. I suffered through utter hell in making that decision, but in the end I emerged with a greater sense of self-worth and security. I am still very careful about telling others that I am gay, and have in fact told only a very few close friends whom I know I can trust. There is really no need to tell my parents at this time. Their reaction would be difficult to predict at best.

Although progression through each successive stage makes the next one that much easier, coming out never becomes the simple statement of self-fulfillment that it should be. It is riddled with social pressures and self-doubt. Perhaps the magnitude of each successive step is only understood when you consider that there is no possible way to return to the closet.

Presently, I am in the midst of the last stage of coming out – becoming active in the gay community. It is both a relief and a terribly frightening experience. Naturally, anyone who is entering unknown territory is going to be frightened at first, but there are a number of ways to approach the matter. I began by becoming as informed about the gay experience as possible through books, films, and other sources. I was careful to select materials done either by gays themselves or by sympathetic or nondiscriminatory groups. After I felt secure enough with myself, I called the local gay community center to inquire about activities in the area. What I discovered was that there wasn't a lot happening outside the bars, but the person on the phone was extremely kind, and we soon became friends. Now, I am beginning to develop a network of gay friends, so I can avoid the bar scenes, which I find distasteful. Nonetheless, the bars could have also provided another option for entering the community. What's most important is that you find a community from which you can gain a sense of support and belonging.

Coming out has been a slow but steady process over the last eight years for me. The road seems never ending. Perhaps it is because life is always changing that we must continually adjust. Or maybe we are given a lifetime simply to discover who we really are, and to help others in the same endeavor. At any rate, the struggle with oneself may never end, but it constantly provides a source of pride as we discover those qualities that make us unique and enable us to enrich the lives of those around us.

▼

Incest is a topic that almost no one wishes to talk about. Both straights and gays are very uncomfortable when discussing the subject. Nonetheless, there are many silent victims of incest, who ache incessantly from facing a personal tragedy in solitude. The horrors of incest are magnified for the gay victim, especially if s/he was violated by a relative of the same sex. Yet, severe problems occur for any incest victim.

In my case, my uncle was the violator. It began at my grandparents' house. I was close to my grandparents, and every weekend for five years I had been making overnight visits to see them.

My uncle had just been released from prison for nonsupport, and he was living with my grandparents. He probably could not find any source of sexual gratification. In addition, he had a severe alcoholism problem and homosexual tendencies to which he would not admit.

One evening, when I was in fourth grade, I was visiting them, and my uncle asked if I knew where babies came from. Naturally, I was only partially correct, so he was going to enlighten me. At first, I caught him off guard, because he wanted to show me pictures of nude women, and I kept hinting that I wanted to see photos of nude men. Don't be misled into thinking that this interest in men gave him incentive. Actually, he severely ridiculed me for showing an interest in men. Contrary to popular belief, my sexual orientation did not make the situation any more pleasant for me. I was silently horrified by his actions. Despite the natural enjoyment of sex, I could nonetheless sense that something was terribly wrong, leaving me with intense guilt feelings. These guilt sensations would cease only years later when I realized that I had nothing to do with these contacts.

I never wanted to go to bed with my uncle, but was caught in an impossible situation. My grandparents had only two bedrooms, so I was forced to sleep with my uncle on the weekends. Besides the problem of having to share a bedroom with my uncle, I was petrified of what he might do if I did not do as he wished. At the time, I did not realize that it was he, not I, who should have feared retaliation. Eventually, I loosened my bond with my grandparents, so as to avoid my uncle but not hurt my grandparents. By eighth grade, I felt I could completely end visiting my grandparents overnight.

That same year I had to endure an extreme personal crisis. My intense feelings of guilt had built to a climax, and I was beginning to discover that other problems were to come. Among the other difficulties I encountered that year was my first episode of school harassment because of my sexuality. Also, I was beginning to withdraw from people and feared sex even with men who interested me (not that I was sexually active or even wanted to be). Finally, to make matters even worse, we had moved into a new neighborhood, quite unlike my formerly protected suburb, and I had problems adjusting. Well, all of these problems ended in five suicide attempts that were cries for help more than they were death wishes. Fortunately, we moved again a year later to another protective suburb, where I was able to straighten out my thoughts and gain some self-respect.

Although I now understand my uncle's actions, I in no way forgive him. Even though I grimace when I think of the times I had sex with him (he was a squalid man – not that it would have made any difference otherwise), I can now deal effectively with my past experiences, and eliminate the grip they had on my life. In fact, I can even laugh sometimes at the absurdity of the whole ordeal.

In twelfth grade, I gave a report on incest to my psychology class. Only three students in a class of thirty knew what incest was in 1980! My teacher told me how happy she was that I was going to deal with the topic of incest. She said, "I'm so glad you're giving a talk on incest, because when I give lectures on subjects like homosexuality and incest, all I can think about is that at least one student in my class is gay or an incest victim or the like. That really scares me." To save her sanity, I never told her that her favorite student was both gay and an incest victim!

If you are an incest victim, you probably feel very isolated and alone. Here are a few suggestions:

1. Try to reason out why the violations may have occurred, to ease your own feelings of guilt. Frequently, you will find that you were used as a last resort for affection, warmth, or sexual release.

2. Read books concerning the topic of incest, such as *Father's Days* by Katherine Brady or *Conspiracy of Silence: The Trauma of Incest* by Sandra Butler.

3. If there is an incest victims' group or clinic where you live, please visit them. However, it is unlikely that support of any kind will be available in your community, so a psychologist or psychiatrist might be in order. When choosing your therapist, be sure that s/he is very open-minded. After all, a therapist who becomes anxiety-ridden when discussing incest cannot help you very much. Don't assume that a gay therapist will be more open-minded when dealing with incest.

4. Analyze how this experience has affected your interpersonal relationships. For example, are you withdrawn? Do you avoid all members of one particular sex? Is the past creating sexual difficulties in the present? Recognizing your problems may bring you one step closer to solving them.

5. Finally, always remind yourself that you are a worthwhile person who deserves respect! Leave yourself messages – even write on your mirror – saying, "I am an attractive person in both personality and appearance."

Just remember that there are others who know your anguish and pain, and wish to ease the sorrow with love, even if we are not there with you.

▼

It is truly sad that so many people find life so unbearable that they attempt to destroy themselves, and even sadder that some succeed. The loss of a single human being is a permanent loss to the world of one person's unique perspective, one person's unique talents, one person's future.

Unfortunately, I found myself staring at pills or a knife on more than one occasion as I came out, and nearly succeeded in destroying myself. I vividly remember the long hours of glaring at the mirror, trying to decide if the image I saw was worth saving. At times, I would just break down and cry. There seemed no end to my problems. A combination of verbal harassment and physical and sexual assault had driven me terribly close to the brink. No one knew the entire reason for my depression. My parents did not know of the physical and sexual abuse, nor did my assaulter know of my problems at school and at home. The lack of compassion and understanding I was experiencing added to feelings of isolation and entrapment. Following an attempt that nearly killed me, my fifth, I decided to fight back and correct my problems rather than be eaten alive by them. It amazed me how little conviction and effort was needed to make major changes in my environment.

There are a few techniques that I found helpful in recovering from my despair. First of all, set some very accessible short-range goals in order to boost your self-image. For example, achieving better grades was one of my short-range goals. Volunteering to help the poor, needy, or handicapped can help instill feelings of self-worth and allow for a reevaluation of the desperation of your own situation. Lastly, leave yourself notes that you are a unique creation offering a valuable contribution to others, and surround yourself with warm, supportive friends.

If you know someone who is going through a crisis, please don't hesitate to offer a friendly ear. Offer support when appropriate, and for God's sake, don't stand idly by and watch a human being self-destruct. Notify a friend or family member of theirs, or suggest professional help to him or her. At any rate, express interest and concern, for each of us is too precious to be lost needlessly, and people need not suffer in isolation and loneliness.

Liza, 17

Los Angeles, California

I had trouble admitting to myself that I was gay, so, for a long time, telling others was out of the question. I had known for quite some time about my sensitive feelings for other girls, but it wasn't until I was seventeen that I first told someone. Somehow, after that, that someone no longer wanted to associate with me. She even turned other friends against me. Unfortunately, ignorance can cause ridiculous behavior.

I live with my father, and he hadn't known about my being gay; he wouldn't have even considered it. But he found out over the holidays. He found out through my cousin, who is gay himself, but ashamed to admit it. Pretty soon, I felt like everyone knew. It was both easy and difficult – easy because I didn't have to face telling anyone, and difficult because most of the people around me were very bigoted, especially my father's girlfriend. She made me go see a therapist, thinking I could be "cured." She laid this crap on me about how gays are all sick in the head. Considering all the years we've known each other, I thought she'd be supportive, but she alienated me for weeks. The tension was really mounting, and I was desperately trying to come up with a solution.

Now the one thing I believe is that a person must be true to him- or herself, but for my own reasons, I had to lie about my being gay. I told her that I was probably just going through a phase. This, you must understand, was to ease the hostility around me. But I knew that it *was* not, and *is* not, a phase.

Since I've been found out (I didn't *come* out), I have been placed under all types of restrictions: no driving the car, not being allowed to see my gay friends, and not being allowed to see my lover. We had to break up – unwillingly, as you can imagine.

Straights and adults say, "How can teenagers know their own minds, let alone know that they're gay?" Well, that is where they're wrong! It's hard, as I'm sure most of us realize, going to school, being gay, and restraining the feelings we want so much to show. Straight friends can't possibly know and can't even begin to understand what it feels like to be gay. As a result, we end up having few friends at school, and our sensitivity about every matter is heightened. There's no escaping the fact that narrow-minded people exist. The best thing is to build your self-confidence in who and what you are. Avoid those who simply cannot deal with "our" issue.

We all have specific difficulties around being gay. My particular hang-up is how to tell a straight friend that she turns me on. An intimate confrontation like that is a delicate affair.

Another thing I'm sure we've all been through, in some form or another, is people telling us, "You're going to be facing a lot of bigoted people," or "How do you know you're *that way?*" (Most people avoid saying the words "gay," "homosexual," or "lesbian.")

My suggestion would be to start some sort of organization, possibly formed by parents of gays, to hold meetings and dances – maybe a membership club. This could be brought about by pinning up bulletins or posters in areas where teenagers hang out, and even though there will be those who will criticize such promotion, I'm positive that at least one out of every seven would take a glimpse and seriously consider it.

The easiest thing to do is get discouraged, and it won't help any if I tell you not to. Try to recapture how happy your gay feelings make you, and how you enjoy being with other gay friends who are like you and know how you feel, or remember how it feels to be with your lover. If you haven't had a lover, well then, you have something to look forward to.

If you had friends that you came out to and they discarded you, I guess you realize they weren't friends in the first place. Get involved with other gays your age. It may be hard at first, but you have to make the effort. Take that first step! And don't hesitate to show how you feel, even if you aren't used to it. You'll get used to it, believe me!! All of a sudden criticism and obnoxious remarks will seem trivial to you.

I'll be glad to get in touch with anyone who wants to write me. We may even start a gay pen pal organization!

Publisher's note: We did! See back of book for details.

Allan, 16

Gillett, Arkansas

I am sixteen and gay. When I started to come out, I told only one straight girlfriend. Later, everyone, including the whole school and town, knew. Many of the boys I knew as friends turned out to be the opposite. They stayed away from me in school and called me "queer," "fag," and "punk." Most of my best friends are girls. I am glad that everyone knows, because as the days go by it gets easier.

I didn't realize I was gay until I was in the fifth grade; I am now in the tenth grade. My first experience came when I'd invited a boy my age to our home. We did nothing more than kiss.

When I first told my girlfriend, I hadn't planned on it. We were going to a basketball game, and there was this guy on the bus who attracted me, so I told her to ask him if I could talk to him. He said nothing, so I never did. I told her because she's very trustworthy and understanding. She wasn't surprised, because she knew of a girl who was this way also.

Everyone else found out about me when I wrote a letter to this same boy about a month later. I dropped the letter by mistake, and another boy, who doesn't like me, found it and told everyone. They talked about it around their parents, and it went on and on.

Afterwards, things got so intolerable, I told my best friend that I planned to take pills. She told my brothers and sisters, and they told my mother about the pills and about how I had written a letter to a boy. My mother said that anyone who likes the same sex is sick. She thought I was mixed up, and she sent me to a counselor. I am still going now, each Monday. I guess my mother realizes things won't change, and she seems to have accepted it. (My father left home when I was born and died six years later.)

Some good has come of all this. My mother and I seem to have gotten closer. People see me the way I am; I'm more myself than I've ever been in my whole life.

But there have been hard parts, too. After my mother found out I was gay, she let me go to Houston to stay with my brother. I guess she thought it would help me get things off my mind. While I was there, I read in the newspaper about a lady who was gay. She was criticizing prejudiced people, and I wrote her and later got her phone number. She called once, and my brother answered the phone. When he realized what was going on, that I really was this way, he sent me home so that his two kids wouldn't be "exposed." I can no longer visit there.

I've lost many of my male friends. Since they know I'm this way, they run off or move quickly if I come near them. I no longer sit with boys in the cafeteria. I sit with girls, because they are the only friends I have. To be honest, I've had more bad experiences than good in coming out.

From the start it was rough, but I had a caring friend to show me the way. Many times I considered running away and even thought about suicide, but then I decided I wasn't going to let other people's criticism run me off or destroy me. There are always going to be people who talk about you or call you names, but there is one thing you can do that will upset them: ignore them.

I am in a town where I am the only person this way. I would like for you to get some of the youngsters to write, if possible. I hope someone out there will write.

D.B., 15

New York City

I'm fifteen years old, and I came out to my mother last fall. She was really puzzled about homosexuality, and she would talk about it like it was some kind of disease. Unfortunately, things at home got worse, and every now and then I wound up not going to school but instead hanging out with a few other young gays.

In October, I moved out of my house to live with a very nice couple that I worked for. I had to run away for a whole week in order to be able to get my mother's permission to move out. My new home was only a block away, and I would come home every day to be with my older sister, who didn't know I was gay, and to pick up my mail. I lived there for about two months. During those two months, I secretly dropped out of school. I could never get along with the students, and some of them thought I was gay. This really bothered me, and it was too much to handle at the time.

In December, I met this guy Reggie, who was twenty-three. I met him hanging out in the subway station. Then things really started going wrong. He spent the night with me a few times, which was okay, but when I started coming in late to work, I was asked to leave. My boss also gave me a two-week notice to start moving my stuff back home. That day I made up my mind: I was no longer going to stay in that neighborhood. I really had a lot of pressure coming down on me from my mother, my family, and the few friends that I had left.

So, with Reggie's help, I moved my stuff to different locations in New York City. Everything was packed in either bags or boxes. I remember struggling on the bus and the subway to reach my friends' houses. I left just about all of my massive wardrobe at my previous lover's apartment, and I didn't go back to get it until two months later.

Anyway, I wound up alternating between Brooklyn and Manhattan, where I lived. Sometimes Reggie and I would have a hard time with our relationship, and lord knows that they were hard times for me especially! I still remember the night I spent the night in a gay movie theatre! Can you imagine paying five dollars just to sleep? Then the next night we slept on the B train between Brooklyn and Manhattan ... The only thing I didn't resort to was hustling. I felt that I was worth more than that and that I'd run the risk of getting caught by an undercover cop.

Before I'd left work, I had saved up about two hundred dollars, because I had worked like a dog those last few weeks. Reggie wasted forty-five dollars of mine buying shirts for himself. I wasted sixty dollars on this phony agency that was supposed to find us a room. Reggie didn't work any of this time, and we were supposed to be living together. I finally broke up with this guy after being taken advantage of and everything else.

Afterwards, in February, I lived with my aunt for about a week. I would go to visit my mother just about every day, because she wanted to talk to me all of the time. She was trying to get me back home, and she wanted me to go with her to family court to do something about the problem. I refused to, as it might have meant living in a group home. After wasting two months of my life, she finally convinced me to go back home. I spent the night for three nights, but I wasn't moving my belongings in fast enough for her. She called the cops and had a warrant out for my arrest. They call it a PINS warrant (Person in Need of Supervision). Anyway, I'll never forget it...

I woke up on a Sunday morning, and just as I was opening my eyes, I heard the rattling of keys, and in come these two policemen telling me to get up and put my clothes on. In the background, my mother was watching, and to make a long story short, they took me away in handcuffs. Can you imagine being brought out of your building with handcuffs on? They took me to the precinct and asked me a few questions and then they told me that since it was Sunday, they would have to send me somewhere to spend the night. I immediately thought of Spofford Juvenile Detention Center in the Bronx. That place is wild! I could get killed!! So I nicely asked the officer if they would try to put me somewhere other than Spofford. I wound up being taken to this place called St. Barnabas House on the Lower East Side of Manhattan. (The other officers immediately started taking orders for lunch, since we would be passing by Chinatown.)

When I arrived there, I was terrified. But it wasn't as bad as I thought it would be. In fact, you could go out until eleven in the evening, and the doors were never locked. If you walked out and didn't come back, you'd get arrested again. The next day at court, my mother was there, and at first she didn't want me back. Luckily, I knew one of the lawyers of the Legal Aid Society, and she straightened things out with me and my mother before we went into the courtroom. The judge didn't want to at first, but he let me go with my mother on probation. I had to meet certain requirements such as going to school, curfew, therapy, and staying at home.

I went back to school, and a few days later I stopped going, because there was still too much pressure for me to work under. I was always quiet and afraid of what other people might think. But I explained to my mother why I really could not attend school, and she understood. So now I don't have to go to school. I got my old job back, and I see my social worker once a week. It really helps, and you don't have to be crazy to go! Today, I am basically a happier person. I guess that bad experiences can really teach you a lot — for better and for worse.

Mark Maki, 18

Minnesota

Hi. I would like to tell you something about myself. I am deaf, gay, and eighteen years old. I grew up in a small town and attended the Minnesota School for the Deaf. I was seventeen when I first realized that I was gay. It took me five or six years to come to this conclusion.

Last summer, I decided to confess to my mother that I was a homosexual. She told me that I should go to see a psychologist, and I did. I think she wanted to cure me of my homosexuality, but it didn't work. My mother and I struggled all year. She seems to be starting to accept me. I hope she will understand my gayness someday.

At school, the boys and girls teased me and called me "fag." They said, "You ought to get married to a man," and laughed at me. I was angry and hurt.

One Sunday, I went to the Lutheran church for the deaf. After the service was over, I decided to talk to the pastor, and I told her I was gay. She understood, and told me about this lesbian couple she knew. She wanted me to meet them, and gave me their address.

They have made me very happy. They talked to me about how the pastor accepted me even though I was gay. They said that many pastors make gays feel bad and guilty. I then prayed to God to accept me as a gay person. I found out that God does accept and love me as His child.

Anyway, the lesbian couple invited me to visit them for a week. They showed me the gay places in Minneapolis. Now I am at St. Mary's Junior College in Minneapolis and am very excited to have gay friends. I would like to have a lover someday.

I believe the handicapped may be gay, too. I have several deaf, gay friends now, and they are very special to me. Good luck, my friends. Take care, and may God bless us as His children.

Jessie, 15

Florida

Iam a fifteen-year-old female bisexual in the tenth grade. I was born in Georgia, but moved to a small town in Florida.

I began thinking about other women when I was in the sixth grade. It was kind of funny. I never had "weird thoughts" before, but when the teacher first walked into the classroom, I got this funny feeling inside. I was attracted to her. I didn't know about my sexuality then.

When I got into seventh grade, I started to realize what being lesbian or gay actually meant. All of my friends had boyfriends, but I was more attracted to the girls in school. That's when I knew I was bisexual. I thought I was weird or different because of it, so I never told anyone about my thoughts.

▼

The summer before my sophomore year was very important. I met one of my mom's friends, and it turned out that she was a lesbian. I started hanging out with her and her girlfriend. They took me to a lot of places where straight people would never go – like lesbian softball games. They taught me how to be free with myself, and not to worry about what other people think. I had a lot of fun with them. They introduced me to a lot of gay men too. I began to hang out with them. We talked about a lot of stuff. They took me to rallies. The gay people there were all so free with themselves. I remember thinking that I wanted to be free with myself, too, but I never had the courage to be. I learned from them that I was no different than anybody else.

That was the summer I told my mom. She was really cool about it. She didn't even care. She told me that she already knew and that it would never stop her from loving me. I figured that since it went so smoothly with my mom, I'd try to tell my sister, whom I love very much. My sister doesn't live at home, and the only way we communicate is through letters. I wrote her a letter saying that I was bisexual. It took her a long time to write back. She avoids the subject of my sexuality, though. I think that she doesn't know how to handle it. She just doesn't know what to say or do, I guess.

This year, my school counselor came right out and asked me if I was gay, so I told her I was bisexual. At first I was really uncomfortable talking about it. But she's really cool. We talk every day. She's helping me deal with people and homophobia, and with ways I can come out and tell everybody. People at school have a lot of assumptions, but nobody knows for sure. Everybody accuses me of being gay. I never say I am or I'm not. Either way, I don't want to be judged by my sexual orientation.

I basically live two lives right now. Soon, I hope, there will be only one. I realize now that if my being bisexual bothers someone, then they don't have to be around me, and I'd rather not be around them. I know that I'm not weird or different. Being gay, lesbian, or bisexual is not a choice. I know that it is the way I was born, and I am proud of what I am.

Jim, 17

Chicago, Illinois

I come from a mixed family: my father is an extremist – status symbols, perfection, etc. – whereas my mother is a conservative – stretches the dollar, and is also a perfectionist. This combination of ideals caused sheer hell when I decided to come out.

It was July, and I had just turned seventeen. I had begun driving *my* car, which I had purchased with *my* money. I already knew my sexual feelings and had accepted them. So I began to use my car and fake IDs to investigate "my world." I had gone to a youth group, but the one I went to was full of hustlers and queens. So I began to go out to bars, porno houses for gays, etc. Many times I really had to speed home to make my midnight curfew. My parents assumed that I was dating someone (a girl), so, at first, they never questioned my going out. But then they got curious and kept bugging me to tell them why and where I was going out. This went on constantly, even on our vacation. They said to tell them and everything would be all right.

Well, it bugs me to hold something back, so the day after we got back from our vacation, I had a conversation with my mom.

"Mom, I always hide something when I'm trying to protect you and Dad. What I mean is, all the times I leave, I've been going on dates with guys, because *I'm gay!!*"

"You cannot be gay ... you don't even know what it means. Do you actually have sex with these people?"

She did not even wait for my answer. She ran to the phone and called up our parish priest. She got no support; he said that gays do exist and, in fact, constitute part of life. This, my mom could not accept. So she called Catholic Charities and made an appointment for a counseling session – for *me,* not for her.

I came out on a Monday, and the appointment was for a Wednesday. On Tuesday, I was tormented at the dinner table by my parents. My dad called me every name in the book while my mom prayed over me, quoting from the Bible. Wednesday came and I was accompanied to Catholic Charities. First, I had a private session and was asked why I was there and what I wanted to accomplish. I said that I wanted to make my parents understand me. Then we had a session with my parents. They weren't there to understand me. They wanted me to go into therapy to be "deprogrammed." But, to their disgrace, Catholic Charities was only interested in how much my dad could "donate" for each session. Of course, this would be calculated according to how much my parents grossed per year.

Wednesday night came and I was at work when I got paged – my mom was waiting for me, because there was a family emergency. I punched out and went to the waiting car.

"What's up?" I asked.

"Just get in the damn car!"

I got into the car and was harassed all the way to our destination. The destination? The office of the principal of my Catholic, all-boys, private high school. He is a vowed Brother, which is like being a priest.

First, I had a session with him. He said, "Tell me everything. This is just like confession. I won't tell your parents. You have my word." I poured out my story to him. I told him everything – bars, dirty bookstores, past lovers, etc. I even told him about the 32-year-old lover that I had at that time. He sounded interested, so when he asked me about gay teachers, I did not hesitate.

Next, he had a session with my parents. Then I was told to come back on Thursday. I went on Thursday, because I thought I had a friend, but I soon found out otherwise. I was told how wrong my lifestyle was, and how I was going to be deprogrammed with the help of a shrink he and my parents picked out.

Well, this was too much for me to take, so I asked my lover if I could move in for four days so I could sort things out. That night I packed, made arrangements for a leave from work, and wrote a letter to my parents explaining my feelings and how much we needed a break to sort things out.

Friday came and I told my mom that I was going shopping. I put the letter in the mailbox as I left. At the suggestion of my lover, I called my principal up to let him know that I was all right. Also at the suggestion of my lover, I called my mom to let her hear my voice and let her know that I was all right. I told my mom I would call her every day and check in.

On Sunday, when I spoke to my parents, they said they wanted to meet me at midnight in a dark parking lot, *alone*. Well, I did not go, because I suspected something.

The fourth day came of my thinking period, and when I called, my parents wanted me to meet them at the principal's office. So I agreed and went. When I got there, I was told how V-neck shirts, gold neckchains, and Adidas shorts were only worn by gay people. Then I was given the conditions of my return:

1. Give up my lifestyle.
2. Like girls.
3. Give up all past friends.

I pondered these conditions for a day and then called and told them that I would be moving in with my lover. A couple of days later, I stopped in before work and packed. I said I would be back to pick up my things that weekend. I was stalling, because I was still hoping everything would work out.

I decided to give them another try and said I would stay overnight one night. I did not tell them I was testing them. When I arrived after work, Dad escorted me to the garage, where I was harassed.

"You fucking queer, you goddamn faggot ... Sissy ... Do you actually have sex with your lover??"

"I don't think it's any of your business."

Grabbing my throat, Dad shouted, "It *is* my fucking business."

I then explained that this was a trial, and since it wasn't working out, I would load my car and leave. They said that would be okay under one condition: that I pull my car into the garage, close the door, load it up, open the door, and leave. This was so the neighbors wouldn't see. (I left my aquarium, my bike, my bird, and a chair, because they would not fit into my car.)

▼

When I got to my lover's apartment, we stored everything at his dad's, as we were going to be moving in a couple of days. I still called my mom every day to let her know how I was doing. The day after we moved, I called my principal and found out that he had traced my phone number and brought my dad and brother to the old apartment to try to find and capture me. But because we had moved, they hit a dead end.

Everything sort of settled down, so I decided I would go back to school. To my disappointment, I found out my parents were holding my school records up, to screw me. I would have to wait another year, until I was eighteen, before they would be released. I accepted this, and decided that I would go to work full-time. I gave my two weeks' notice at my old job, but got a surprise before the two-week period ended. I was getting off work, and my parents cut me off while I was on my way to my car. "We want to talk," they said. I thought this would all be finally settled, so I got into the car.

"We cannot handle you anymore, so you are being committed. As for your lover – he's in jail for contributing to the delinquency of a minor." (This was not true – yet.)

I was driven to Christ Community Hospital, where police met me so I wouldn't run away. They told the admitting clerk that I was suicidal and a drug addict. There was no room in the hospital, so I was transferred to Forest Park Institution. And guess who showed up in the ambulance?? My good old principal, who, by that time, had told my parents everything that I had told him.

When I got to the hospital, everything was taken, except my clothes – so I wouldn't kill myself. Then I was strip-searched and questioned until five in the morning. They let me sleep until seven, and then got me up for a blood test and a regular day with the patients.

I got a passport book in which punches were recorded every time I did something without a hassle. You could redeem these for cigarettes or candy, or you could buy status levels with them. When telephone privileges were granted, I phoned a friend of my lover's to let him know where I was. A regular day included group sessions where we would beat tennis rackets on cushions to relieve our anxiety. We also outlined our bodies and drew our features in, played Uno, etc.

During one of these days, I was given some educational tests: the first one consisted of building with blocks; the second, picture interpretation. (What does this ink blotch remind you of?) The third test was for reading comprehension, and the fourth was a math quiz.

The second day of my ten-day stay, I was sent for a physical, where the doctor finger-fucked me. The third day, I talked to a lawyer that my lover had gotten for me. Then I signed what's called a "five-day," which was the quickest possible way for me to get out. The doctor had five days to prove before a court that I was insane. If he couldn't, I would be released.

It happened that my parents came to visit on the day my lawyer came to talk to me. They began harassing me, and my lawyer, as well.

"Is he a fucking faggot, too?" they asked me. They told my lawyer, "You shouldn't represent him; he has no money."

My lawyer explained that money was not his concern, at which point my father said, "Oh, then he's your fucking whore."

My lawyer tried to reason with them, but they stormed out, saying, "We'll see you in court."

I endured those next days awaiting the doctor's decision. Then, right before I would have gone to court, the doctor dropped my case. Now where to go? My parents did not want me. They did not want me with my lover, and they did not want me with my relatives. Finally, I was given a temporary three-week placement with the perfect family: Catholic, house in the suburbs, station wagon, two kids, etc. In order for me to get out, my parents had to sign a release. They let me sit though Labor Day weekend before coming to do it. Then I was released to my new family – after ten days of confinement.

The family was really kind to me, but after one week I decided I did not like the idea of being pushed from home to home. I went to my mom and told her I was moving in with my lover again. (I picked up my bird and the aquarium. They had changed the locks on the house, and my mom waited until I left before going to a scheduled engagement.)

I moved in with my lover and got a full-time job. My records were still being held up, so I planned to finish high school when I turned eighteen. All I needed were two more credits.

I had a seventeen-year-old friend who knew my mom. During this time, he landed in the hospital with bleeding ulcers. Mom called his mother and told her about me, saying that my being gay was the cause of his illness. My friend rejected me for a time, but it all worked out.

I gave my mom my phone number and P.O. box number. Then I began getting mass cards and religious articles. I disregarded them, just as I had disregarded the copies of the Ten Commandments I had found in my clothing with "Thou shalt honor thy father and mother" and "Thou shalt not commit adultery" underlined. An example of what I received was a pamphlet from an unfortunate-men's home in Wisconsin. My mom added to the pamphlet, "Jim, if you are too ashamed to come home, go to the Blessed Mother."

There were private detectives following me around. One even came up to me and told me that I should listen to my parents. The others silently followed me, or cruised me, and laughed hysterically when they got my attention. But I was so emotionally broken down that I couldn't believe my parents would bother me anymore, and I paid no attention to them.

Then on Friday, the thirteenth of October, private investigators picked up my lover and came to the apartment, where I was, and tore it apart. My parents had told them we were running a drug and porno ring. All they found was my asthma medication and bay leaves. My lover and I were hauled down to the station. I was interrogated alone and then in front of my lover. Finally, I was turned over to my parents, and charges were pressed against my lover. I was to live with my parents for two weeks, until my court date. I left the station with my parents, but when I got into the car, I was held down and beaten up until my face was a pool of blood. I couldn't get out of the car, so I had to endure this until we got to my house. (I was told in the car that I had to give up my possessions and would be readmitted on Monday to another mental institution.) As soon as we got out of the car, I fled to the police station — still bloody. I filed a battery report against my dad but found out it could not be enforced, because he beat me in Chicago and we were now in Oak Forest.

The police called my parents, assuring me that nothing else could happen. When my parents came, everything went well until I asked to phone my lawyer. My dad went into a rage. The police saw what I had been going through and would not release me to my parents. So my lawyer drove all the way out at two in the morning to pick me up. He was assigned as my guardian until the court date. I had to live with a friend, because I was banned from my apartment. During this time, my parents went through two lawyers and bugged the police so much that they offered to testify in my behalf.

The first court date came, and the case was continued. On the second one, I was put on supervision. It was determined that I could live where and with whomever I wanted to. My parents never showed up at my lover's court dates, so the charges were dropped.

I began to make contact with my other relatives only to find that my parents had told them their side of the story. They had done such a good job that most of my relatives wouldn't talk to me.

In February, I got my bike and my chair. I had had a silver-dollar collection worth over one thousand dollars, but my parents sold it to pay for their bills. My supervision was terminated, because I was back at school and still had my full-time job.

Here it was, one month before my eighteenth birthday, and everything was still going full steam. I had visited one of my aunts and my grandmother to show them that I was still the same person. So, one weekend, I decided to surprise my grandparents and went for a visit, bringing my new lover with me. It just so happened that my two aunts came up with their families, too. The first two days went extremely well, but then my uncle threatened to leave if my grandparents did not get rid of the two queers. So my grandparents told me it was all right if I visited them alone, but they did not want to meet any of my friends. They had talked to a Catholic priest, who told them the "demon" works through gay people.

My grandma had a civil conversation with my lover before we left, then twisted the story when she talked to my mom. The next thing I know, I get this letter from my mom:

Dear Son,

I feel I must warn you. They are programming you for suicide. Your lover told your grandma that if we (the family) do not accept you, you would take your life.

Jim, if you are happy with your lover, why do you look for acceptance? I'll tell you why. Because you and your lover do not have true love. You have selfish love and sympathy for one another. You will never be happy being a homosexual and you proved it. You are living like an animal; going from one to another. What ever happened to ———, ———, and who knows how many more?

You wanted independence. What happened? You have your freedom and you still come back to the family.

God help you because you cannot help yourself. They are controlling your life.

Love, Mom

I am grateful that I have such a caring person as my lover. It gives me the courage to cope with things like this letter. I used to let it bother me, but I looked at everything that I have and realized how lucky I am. I am proud of my accomplishments, and that is all that matters to me.

DeMelon Faith, 19

South El Monte, California

About four years ago, I figured out that I was attracted only to females. I was fifteen at the time. Every other day I would go to the Tastee Freeze to grab an ice cream after tennis practice. I noticed this really cute girl there and decided I wanted to get to know her as a friend. It turned out we were both freshmen at my school. We never had classes together, but we grew to be friends, and wrote letters and passed them through other friends. We were buddies till the end.

One day the following summer, Mia and I went on a long bike ride together. We got home at about five p.m. and went to her house. We were tired and just wanted to relax and listen to the radio. All of a sudden Mia started messing around, giving me a backrub. One thing led to another, and we discovered something even more exhausting than bike riding. This lasted the whole summer and half of our sophomore year. We both agreed we would never tell anyone. We were convinced we weren't like "real lesbians."

But after the first semester of my sophomore year, I began to show my feelings more strongly. I think this made Mia very uncomfortable. (I didn't hear her say she was uncomfortable when we spent the night together, though.) So, I got upset. First she told me we weren't like other lesbians, that we were different. Then she had to tell our friends one day that we weren't boyfriend and girlfriend. (We weren't boyish-looking girls; we were feminine.) Suddenly I saw how cruel she could be. I'd fallen in love with her, and she laughed in my face, right in front of her friends, saying we weren't a couple.

After that, if I thought anyone liked me, I blew them off. I became celibate. I even thought of becoming a nun. Now that I'm older, though, I'm glad that she was in my life. She's the only sexual experience I've had to this day. I've had a hard time telling or trusting anyone about my sexuality because of what happened with Mia. It's discouraging to be a lesbian these days because of all the homophobia. I admit I'm afraid and I'm still in the closet.

I haven't told my family or my friends. They're all Roman Catholic ... I think some of them might start wearing a garlic necklace if I told them. Am I supposed to feel ashamed of being gay and in the closet?

Deborah, 18

Los Angeles, California

My name is Deborah. I'm a senior in a Los Angeles County high school. I am also gay. Although I figured out that I was gay the summer I was sixteen, I didn't admit it to myself for a year and a half. I knew that I wasn't interested in boys when I was sixteen. I was in love with an older female friend who was thirty-six and married. We'd go out as friends, but I'd feel a lot more for her than she did for me. Once, she caught me spying on her. She asked me if I thought I might be gay. My first reaction was, "Who, me? I'm too young to be gay. I'm sure it's only a stage."

Over the months, I realized that it wasn't a stage. I discovered that I had no feelings for boys, and that was all my friends used to talk about. I realized that the subject of boys was boring to me. I knew that I was gay then, because I was eighteen and I didn't know one other eighteen-year-old, twelfth-grade girl who didn't like boys.

My first gay contacts were made in gay groups of Alcoholics Anonymous, which I belong to. I also joined a lesbian rap group at UCLA. I found out about this through a friend who goes to UCLA. I contacted the Gay Center in Hollywood and am attending a class there. I also made some contacts and met my first lover through an organization called the League, where contact is made by mail.

At first the word "lesbian" sounded negative to me. It was used as a put-down by my peers and family. I also was very confused by the stereotypes of lesbians. I used to think that I had to wear guys' clothing, but now I know that that was only a stereotype. Now I realize that being lesbian doesn't mean I have to look or dress any particular way.

I tried to come out to my mom two months ago, but she thinks it is a stage. She tells me, "When I was young, I didn't like boys either; you'll grow out of it." I am an only child, so naturally, she has hopes that I'll get married and have grand-children "for her." I told her that that notion was rather selfish and that there was no law that required me to get married and have children. She often pressures me about guys, and I either tell her that she is boring me or I ignore her. Personally, I think she'll accept it when she is ready.

I would like to give some advice on how to tell your friends about being gay. First of all, don't tell just anyone. You have to really trust someone in order to tell them. You must observe a person for a long time to see if they are someone you should tell. It is best not to tell people who are prejudiced, overly religious, or immature. Before telling someone, it is best to find out their general opinion of the subject. The best time to bring it up is when the subject of sex or marriage is being discussed. I've basically gotten three reactions:

1. "It's no big deal, just don't try anything on me" (if they are female).

2. "Eeew – Gross!! You're disgusting."

3. "You are a sinner."

All but one person that I've told are still my friends. They don't bring it up, but sometimes we all joke around about it. They don't intend to hurt me, though. Many times, they can't relate to my talking about girls the way they talk about guys. Sometimes it freaks them out, but they are still my friends.

Often I am paranoid in the presence of this guy that I know. I told him, and he is not my friend anymore. I see him at school, but, so far, nothing has been said.

It really isn't as big a deal as most teenagers make it out to be. On the bus, people are always telling "fag" jokes. I usually ignore them. Not everyone in my life has to know — it is my business, and that is what's important.

Rick Cary, 24

Chapel Hill, North Carolina

Coming out means different things to different people. For me as a gay man, it refers to a long process of self-discovery that led me to realize and celebrate my sexuality. It also refers to my telling others that I'm gay. My coming-out process led me to say to myself and others, "I'm gay and proud."

I was a "late bloomer." My sexual awareness dawned more slowly than it did for many folks. During high school, I thought certain boys were good-looking; I worried about having an erection in the locker room. But I didn't think this was unusual. I figured all boys admired an attractive male body.

I don't think I had heard the word "gay," only "fag." What I had heard about them was negative, and I certainly didn't feel like a pervert. I knew no one who was gay, and no one questioned my assumed heterosexuality. I dated girls and went steady a few times, but I never loved any of them. Still, I didn't think I was different from other guys, until...

One day, while a senior, I was in a shopping mall bookstore and saw a magazine that included a picture of a naked man modeling jewelry. I liked what I saw. Thinking it to be a magazine for men, I bought a copy. Later, to my surprise, I read on the cover that it was "a magazine for women"! I then began to suspect that I was not like other boys. Something about me was different; my self-discovery had begun.

I entered college at a major state university as a naïve eighteen-year-old from a small southern town. I had yet to meet a homosexual, but that was to change. I met Jerry, a member of a campus gay organization who spoke to my psychology class. Although I cannot remember his words, I do recall his presence. Blond and attractive, he sat on a table's edge, his legs swinging freely as he spoke comfortably about being gay. Being gay no longer seemed unimaginable. He was no stereotype, but flesh and blood. Like me. And I began to wonder: Am I gay?

The summer following my freshman year provided an emotional turning point. I worked in a hamburger joint with Pete, a guy from high school. His eyes and smile captivated me, and I recall that he'd occasionally touch my arm and pat my behind. I loved to be with him, and when I returned to college in the fall, I thought of him constantly. I was nineteen and had never felt so warmly about anyone. But I never told him I loved him. I couldn't; it was too scary. Yet my love for him added fuel to a fire that was lighting a path toward my sexual awareness.

Throughout college, I struggled to understand my sexuality. Was I going through a "homosexual phase"? What did my feelings mean? I struggled to understand the implications of being gay. Was being gay a sign of psychological sickness or immaturity? Was homosexuality a sin? My many questions boiled down to two: Am I gay? Is being gay okay?

I needed help to sort things out. So I read a lot of books on homosexuality from psychological and Christian perspectives. I also talked with a psychologist and several ministers who accepted me. They let me explore my sexual feelings honestly. They supported me as I wrestled to understand not only my sexuality, but myself as a human being.

When I started my senior year, I was still unclear about my sexuality. I had dated women with increasing frequency, but never felt love for any of them. I discovered that I could perform sexually with a woman, but heterosexual experiences were not satisfying emotionally. I felt neither love nor emotional oneness with women. Indeed, I had concluded that I was incapable of human love.

During that year, I again experienced love like I had felt for Pete. Stephen was a hallmate, and I was drawn to him physically and emotionally. I longed to be with him. We teased each other, but I was afraid to tell him of my love. My feelings for Stephen provided more fuel for the fire.

At the age of twenty-one, I looked at the evidence in my life. I realized that the only people I had loved were men, and now I loved Stephen. During college, my gay feelings had grown increasingly strong; my sexual fantasies and dreams were about men. Although I had not had sex with a man, I knew how I felt. Through counseling and reading, I became able to say, "Gay is good." I realized that being gay is neither a sickness nor a sin. During my final semester, after four years of conscious struggle, I was able to say, "I am gay and proud."

I went to my first gay dance (was I scared!) and had a wonderful time. Right after graduation, I met Stuart. We fell in love, and for the first time I shared love and sex with a man. I felt whole and at peace with myself and with God. Finally, I had come to see my sexuality with clarity. I could affirm and celebrate my gayness. I had come out.

My coming out includes telling others I'm gay. Some gays tell everybody, but that's not my style. I have chosen to be selective in telling others. The Bible says, "Do not throw your pearls before swine, lest they trample them underfoot and turn to attack you." Well, my gayness is one of my treasured pearls, a pearl I own after paying a great price of personal struggle. I won't share that treasure with everybody. However, I have come out to many folks whom I care about and with whom I have significant relationships.

Most of the nongay people who know I'm gay are friends. I began coming out to friends while a senior in college. Coming out was scary then ... and still is! I never know how someone will react to my gayness. Some friends suspected all along; others were totally surprised. Some said, "So what?"; others were upset. I've told several dozen friends and none have rejected me. Oh, many have struggled to understand my gayness, but they were willing to struggle. And my coming out has often led to deeper, more open relationships. I've been fortunate; other gays have experienced more rejection than I have.

Over the years, I've learned a few things about how to come out to someone. I need to tell my friend that I want to share something very personal, something that she or he may not understand at first. I want my friend to know that I desire a deeper friendship. I need to avoid coming out when I'm angry with someone. I want my coming out to be an act of love: the sharing of a treasured pearl with a friend. I also remind myself that an initial reaction of disbelief or anger is common. If my friend is upset, he or she may need time to wrestle with my gayness. I can offer to be there and answer questions (and often there are lots of questions!), but I cannot make my friend accept me. Every time I come out to someone, I risk losing that friend. With each individual, I decide if I want to take the risk.

Perhaps nothing is riskier than coming out to parents. I came out to my parents at the same time I came out to myself, but I wasn't prepared for their reaction. How I wish I could have read the Switzers' book *Parents of the Homosexual* before I came out to them. I could have had more realistic expectations, for the Switzers described my parents' reactions with amazing accuracy.

Mom and Dad first reacted with disbelief. "You can't be gay! You must be mistaken." They were so upset, they sent me back to school and said, "Don't come back home until we say you can." Those were the most painful words I've ever heard. For a brief moment I considered suicide, but I had friends and ministers to turn to for support. I was not alone.

After a few weeks, they re-established contact with me. They realized they could not run from the issue. After the initial shock, they felt a flood of emotions. *Anger.* They were angry with me for causing them so much pain and for refusing to see a psychiatrist. They were angry with everyone who might have "made" me gay – college friends, the ministers who counseled me, and, finally, themselves. They felt guilty and wondered, "How did we fail?" *Fear.* They knew it's tough being gay in our society, and they feared I was throwing away my college education and promising future. *Sadness.* The "little Ricky" they knew was no longer the same. Their expectations for me, especially a wife and children, were suddenly taken away. Much had changed, and they grieved for the loss of their dreams for my life ... and their lives too.

That's a lot of heavy emotion, and I felt emotional too. I was angry with them for their reaction. I feared for my future and felt sad that our relationship was strained. The first year was incredibly tense, so tense that it was often terribly uncomfortable for us to be together. We have talked some about my gayness, but we most often avoid the topic. It's scary for all three of us. Yet we need to struggle with each other and our relationships. Happily, they have often demonstrated their love for me in recent years. I am still their son, and our lives go on.

Thus far in my life, I have come out selectively, but one day I may decide to come out very publicly as some gays have done. A part of me wants to do that, but for now I choose otherwise. Each gay must make his or her choice. Coming out, to oneself and to others, is an intensely personal and individual experience. Each coming-out story is unique. This has been mine, but the story has not ended, because I am continually coming out. I will always need to reaffirm the goodness of my gayness and share that pearl with people I care about. I am coming out.

Mark Holmes, 18

Willow Grove, Pennsylvania

I had gay feelings very early in life. I can remember wanting to kiss and touch other boys since I was five or six. Other boys would get embarrassed when I tried to kiss them. I never understood what the attraction was, but I learned to accept it. I thought about boys very often, but I also had crushes on girls in second grade. Now I think about boys almost exclusively.

Although I knew I was "different" very early on, I never talked about it at all until I was eighteen. I was silent about it for at least thirteen years.

The first people I came out to were the people who worked the Gay Switchboard Counseling Service in nearby Philadelphia. The two people I talked to helped me to realize I was not alone. Dottie and Bill gave me a lot on those lonely nights when I called the switchboard. I am deeply thankful that they were there to talk to.

Another big step in my coming out was my first couple of visits to Giovanni's Room, and to the Philadelphia Gay Youth Group. Giovanni's is the biggest gay bookstore in the country and maybe the biggest in the world. The first few times I went there, I went secretly. I soon fell in love with one of the workers there, and became friends with some of the others. I felt very much afraid when I first walked into Giovanni's. I entered the store and knocked over stacks of books. But the people there were friendly and patient. Giovanni's Room has a special place in my heart.

On the first day at the Philadelphia Gay Youth Group, my stomach was a bundle of nerves. I didn't know what to expect. Would these people like me? Would I meet anyone I knew from school? My friend Skip gave me the encouragement I needed, and I walked into the smoke-filled room in the Gay Community Center totally afraid, but expecting to have a good time. I did.

I have been going now for five months. The group meets Saturdays from one to three o'clock, and twenty or thirty people come. The group consists of both men and women, blacks and whites. Some topics we have discussed include coming out, straight friends, parents, lesbian mothers, relationships, gay friends, sex, heterosexuality, suicide, transsexuals, self-defense against rape, racism and sexism in the community, the draft, the bars, separatism, and everything else that relates to our lives.

After the support meetings, the group has done club activities such as drama clubs and poetry meetings. In the drama clubs, we act out skits about unusual situations or pretend to be objects. We are planning to publish our poetry in book form. The biggest project now planned is going to the Christopher Street Liberation Day Rally in New York. We also planned an anniversary prom to celebrate our first birthday. As a friend to the Youth Group has said, young gays are "pioneers." We are the future of the gay movement and community.

Although I am out in the community, I have chosen to remain closeted at school. This is not to say that people don't suspect. I have even thought of wearing a t-shirt that says, "I know you know." A friend, Liz, once compared being gay in high school to the experience of wetting your pants in second grade. "Everyone moves away from you." Sometimes the loneliness can be very painful. Many people will not deal with me because I am gay. I know of no other gay people in school — men or lesbians, students or teachers.

But my high school career as token queer will soon be over. I will graduate in three weeks. This will allow me to be more active in the gay community and to establish more relationships. Graduation will also allow me to achieve personal growth. After twelve years of being hassled in school, I will feel a new kind of freedom.

I sometimes wonder how I survived the hostile, macho attitudes against gay people that I've had to deal with five days a week. Despite this, I am learning to be proud about being gay.

▼

I have recently celebrated the nine-month anniversary of my coming out to my parents. I came out to my parents the night after Christmas. I began with, "I have something to tell you." My mother immediately asked, "You mean you're getting married?"

"Well, Mom, not exactly."

Needless to say, they were shocked. My mother's first words were, "I don't believe you." My father's reaction was to tell me that I wasn't gay, just confused. He told me that young people are often unsure of their sexual identity, and that lots of kids think they're something that they're not — going through stages and all that.

That night I got to tell my parents many of the things that I had newly found out. I talked to my parents about love, stereotypes, the gay community, relationships, and religion. The main concern of my parents was my safety and well-being. At the time, the news was focusing a lot on John Wayne Gacey, the man accused of murdering dozens of teenage boys, and so the case was on my parents' minds. Often the media is guilty of finding only the negative side of anything vaguely involving homosexuality. I tried to teach my parents what most gays were like and that murder and violence were no more a part of gays' lives than of straight people's lives. I think I succeeded in educating my parents and dispelling some of their fears to a certain extent.

It is interesting to notice how my parents' attitudes have changed since I came out to them, and how I have changed and matured. My mother has grown more supportive of me and less fearful of the gay community. She is growing to be more sensitive to my gay feelings and more accepting of my gay friends. She has even had many friendly phone conversations with my gay friends. For Mom, this is quite an achievement. I understand her initial fear and apprehension about the unknown world of homosexuals because of her conservative background and upbringing.

Although Mom has grown more supportive of me, my father has grown less so. Dad now refuses to deal with homosexuality and cannot relate to my sexuality. We haven't talked about it in a long time and maybe never will discuss it again. I understand my dad's feelings about me and my sexuality. I can imagine why he is homophobic and why he is against gays who are out. For a man of his age and background, this is to be expected. I accept his attitudes, and I am no longer trying to change him. I realize that my father's feelings toward me as a son have not changed.

Chrissy, 16

New Jersey

I've always had feelings for the same sex. About two years ago, I realized I was a lesbian. I was scared of so many things. I was especially scared that my family and friends would find out and reject me. I wanted to fit in so badly that I went out with guys. I was trying to please everyone but myself. Then I decided to stop torturing myself, and I stopped seeing guys. I haven't come out to my friends yet, but I'm sure some of them have their suspicions.

My family found out last year when my mother realized that my friend was actually a girlfriend. She's having a rough time dealing with this. She denies that I'm gay and believes someone talked me into it. She thinks I'm too young to know. She had high hopes for me. She wanted me to get married and have children. She tells me I'll be straight once I find the right guy.

It's been difficult to meet other gay teens. I sometimes feel like I'm the only one. I know of some support groups, but I don't want to go alone.

Kenneth, 17

Moorhead, Mississippi

I've known I was different since I was five or six. At that time, I didn't understand the feelings inside me or what they meant. I just knew that I was attracted to boys. I had no idea that people were hated for liking and loving people of the same sex. I thought that everybody liked boys. To this day, I can't believe I was that naïve!

As I grew older, I began paying attention to the stories on the news. I would see people protesting and shouting things like "queers," "fags," "dykes," and "homos." It really hurt and scared me to see people preaching hate like that. They just assumed that if you're gay you must be a pervert or some kind of sexual deviant. From then on, I knew to keep my sexuality a secret.

Then the AIDS crisis began. All of the reports on TV in the mid-'80s said that many gays were being killed by this disaster. I thought that just because I was gay, my chances of getting the disease would be higher than if I was straight. (Later I learned that there is no high-risk group, just high-risk behavior. That was very comforting!)

I fell apart during my freshman year of high school. I sank into a deep depression, and at times I was very suicidal. I eventually dropped out, because I could not cope. My parents wanted to know what was wrong with me. They would ask tons of questions. I wanted to tell them the truth, but I couldn't. I became withdrawn from life. All I did was stay in bed and ask God, "Why me?"

I started smoking, and I ate myself into oblivion. I stopped doing everything and going anywhere. I lived in my bedroom, coming out only when my family was gone or asleep. I lived this way for the better part of two years. All that time I spent alone, all I could think about was my sexuality. I was trying to figure out what I had done to deserve this hell. I just knew I must have done something bad and God was punishing me. I thought that, because I was gay, I didn't deserve happiness and that I was not worthy of anything positive. It got so bad that I was considering suicide as my way of getting out. I wanted to die.

One night, I was home alone and decided to reach out and find help. I called the only number I could find. It was a hotline for runaways. I told them I was gay and that I needed help. They referred me to a gay and lesbian teen crisis line. I called and talked to a counselor for two hours. The person I spoke to told me that I was okay and that I was not alone. They sent me some information about gay teens. I learned the world is full of people like me, people who have gone through what I was going through. People who cared.

My recovery was slow. But it happened. I got back everything I had lost – my self-esteem. I was finally feeling whole again. As I came out of my depression, I decided that I needed someone on my side. I had to tell someone. That someone was my sister, who was living with my family at the time. It took me four months to get my nerve up to tell her. Finally, one day when we were home alone, I just did it. I told her I was gay. I expected a negative reaction. She just looked at me for a few seconds, and then she said that she'd always known I was different. We talked for the rest of the day. About everything. We laughed and cried, too.

I took a big risk telling my sister, but everything changed for the better when I came out to her. She is very supportive. Whenever I'm feeling bad about something pertaining to my sexuality, I have someone to go to. She's there for me. She doesn't judge. She listens and offers advice on how to cope. Now I don't have to keep all of those bad feelings inside me. I can get them out, deal with them, and move on. My sister is so supportive that gay jokes bother her more than they do me!

I don't know any other gay teens yet, but I do have a couple of pen pals who live in other states. We discuss everything from politics to sex.

In closing, I just want to say that deep inside I know the day is coming when gays, lesbians, and bisexuals will not have to hide. We must continue to stand up for ourselves and let everyone know that we are normal people. We are not second-class citizens, and we won't be treated like we are. Right now, I'm in the process of earning a high school diploma through a home-study course. I'm planning to go to college. I realize that I'm gay, I'm proud, and I'm gonna get mine!

James Brock, 24

Seattle, Washington

The most difficult problem created by my homosexuality was having to deal with the religious beliefs I was raised with. Dealing with these was harder than the years of being called names, the years of being rejected by my peers, and the time spent trying to regain the understanding of my family.

My religious roots are both Pentecostal and Baptist. Either of these alone would have been enough to have caused me severe mental problems, but with the two combined, and my homosexuality on top of it all, I wonder how I actually managed to make it this far with any feelings for God intact at all!

I accepted most of the rules and ideals set forth by both of these denominations. I taught Bible school and Sunday school, and led the singing for both the children's and the adult church services. I understood the idea and concept of such practices as "Ye must be born again" and speaking in tongues while in prayer. It was made perfectly clear in both of these churches that:

1. Yes, homosexuals existed.
2. Homosexuals were damned to eternity in Hell.
3. Homosexuals had no place in society.

Of course, I never asked about homosexuality, or even connected what they were talking about with the fact that I was sexually attracted to other males. I always thought of homosexuals as old men who walked poodles on rhinestone leashes and wore makeup. I never thought, dreamed, or realized that there were, or ever had been, homosexuals who were my age. Since my first sexual awareness at about age ten, I knew that I was sexually excited by men. Not until about the age of fifteen did I begin to realize that the people I had heard damned time and time again — the people my religious leaders saw as such destroyers of morality — and I were the same. I was one of them.

It both angered and frightened me. It frightened me because I now thought I was doomed to Hell. It angered me because I felt that all of the church work I had done had been done for nothing, and that somehow God had let me down and allowed my soul to be taken by the Devil.

I tried to change myself. I prayed every day to have a sexual feeling for girls. I prayed that I would start liking sports. I prayed that I would stop watching sports just so I could look at the guys. But no change ever came.

Religion had been my lifeline, my stronghold, the one thing I was good at. On the ballfield, I was always the last picked for all of the teams. Then I would proceed to lose the games by dropping the pop-fly or easy-out ball. Not purposely — I just could not get into the spirit of the games. And after years of verbal abuse, I had no desire to try and improve my gamesmanship. But in church! I was a whiz at leading the songs, helping with the offerings and communion, teaching. And now I felt that I no longer had anything I was "good" at, and that I was no longer loved and protected by a God I had devoted my life to. My prayers had always been my secret solace, and now I felt I was just talking to the wind.

For over five years, although I still remained as active and involved in my church programs as ever, I was only going through the motions. I still believed in God, but I had no real feeling that God believed in me.

I was twenty before I found the feeling of God's love again. I was just finally accepting my sexuality, and facing the fact that while I was going to Hell, life was still going on. I decided to confide my woes to my best friend. I had grown up with him and trusted him; besides, I could no longer hide my feelings about my sexuality and needed a release. To my utter astonishment, he in turn told me that he also was gay and had been dealing with these same problems of "God rejection." I was more fortunate than most in having this happen to me, as my friend was able to introduce me to a very wise and wonderful pastor who opened my eyes, and helped me re-open my heart. Together, he and I read the Scriptures that had plagued my life. He pointed out that each of them could be read to say what anyone wanted it to say. He showed me how beliefs differed from religion to religion. And that it was my accepting what man had been saying rather than accepting the feeling of love and peace I had felt before that was causing my pain and feeling of excommunication from God. As he said, I had been given life by God, and these feelings were a part of the Whole Me that God had created. After talking with him, I began to realize that I had allowed my life to change and be ruled by mere bigoted ideas and ignorance. I was still the same person I had always been, and God loved me as much then as He did when I was ten. It was such a relief to know that I could be a Christian who was gay, rather than just accepting the fact that I was gay and trying to be a Christian.

Religion and religious beliefs can be as strong as the sexual urges facing an adolescent; at least in my case, they were. The question of whether or not to have sex is one thing, but the dilemma of wanting a type of sex for which you are told there is no forgiveness by God can be devastating. It is hard enough to deal with the taunting, the jeers, and being ostracized by your peers. But when your religion, the one and only security you have come to know, turns you away, the hollow emptiness cannot be filled in any way.

It is unfortunate that everyone is not as understanding and caring as the person I was able to talk with. It is also unfortunate that by the time most young people discover their own sexuality, be they gay or straight, their religious mores and values are pretty well set. To someone talking with a young gay person who is confused with the conflicts of their religion and their sexuality, I would first suggest that they convey the fact that they were created and loved by their God before they became aware of their sexuality, and that that has not changed. What has changed are the sexual values and feelings in their lives. They must try to take the time to understand that they, like every other person who has ever lived, must deal with their religious feelings first of all within their own soul. Then, as I mentioned before, they must read their own Scriptures and find that these can be read in many different ways, and that they must read and apply them to their lives as a person who is first and foremost a Christian, Catholic, Jew, whatever, and then as a homosexual. It is in this manner that I regained the spiritual part of my life that I thought was lost forever.

I am hardly a theologian or a student of the seminary. I am a 24-year-old college student. My lover is 21, and devotion and worship of God has been an important part of our relationship for the past three years. Maybe my ideas and story are meaningless to most, but if they can help even one person to avoid the torment that I faced, then they have accomplished something.

Brandon Carson, 17

New Mexico

I like who I am. I have come to accept myself on psychological as well as physical terms. I not only like myself, I like everyone around me. Today, for some gays and especially our youth, that is really hard to say. To learn to accept yourself as you are, and then to start liking yourself completely, is an obstacle some people never overcome. That alone is tough, but to finally do that and then start living a complete and fulfilling life is really too much, isn't it? Is it really too much to ask for us to be able to go out into society and hold jobs and pursue careers and live the "American Dream"? Should we stay closeted and have to hide our feelings, forever living in a make-believe world, hoping that no one finds out about us? The pressure is inevitably on at full force, and even the smallest decisions could radically change our lives.

When I realized I was homosexual, the first thing I did was sit down and cry. I wept for myself, but mostly I cried because I didn't conform. I couldn't be this way, because it "just wasn't right." I wondered why the same sex attracted me and why I felt desires that I knew I shouldn't. After I came to terms with my sexuality, I decided to sequester my feelings, if not for my sake, at least for the sake of my loved ones. I decided to try dating, and I explored the drawers where my father hoarded his *Playboy*s. If my "naturalness" wasn't going to come by itself, then I was ready to force it upon myself. I delved into anything manly. I registered for Little League baseball, Boys' Club basketball, and all kinds of sports. I started reading books about cars and engines. I stopped hanging around with my older sister. I really did some drastic things – all of which I hoped would make me do a complete turnaround and become a heterosexual.

I was fair in sports – no Reggie Jackson or "Magic" Johnson, but I played my positions adequately enough. I talked just as foul as all the other guys in the locker room, and I even hung up centerfold pictures in my locker. But that secret urge to watch all the boys during showers always crept back to haunt me. I always made sure I was the last to shower, and I showered alone, for fear of the worst – an erection. After gym class, I would always hang out with the guys and take part in their open lust for the opposite sex, but all the while I was tearing my mind up wondering about myself.

At this time, I was fifteen and had never gone out with a girl, and some of my friends were beginning to notice this. One of my closest buddies decided to "help" me out and set me up with a nice-looking girl. I hesitantly agreed to the date and actually found myself somewhat elated at the prospect of possibly "getting laid." Well, I went on the date, and time seemed to move by hurriedly. First to a movie, out to eat ... then what? The girl knew I was somewhat introverted, so she made the first moves and asked me if I would like to go to the park. I agreed, and we drove out there. We sat under a large oak tree and she put her arms around my body and moved very close to me. Gosh, this was foreign to me. A girl making the first move – what was I supposed to do? She started talking about something trivial, I can't remember what, and out of the blue she placed her lips upon mine and started kissing me. She opened her mouth and tried to get me to open mine. After she was unsuccessful at arousing me, she asked me what was wrong. I made up some stupid excuse and said I had to go home. She took this personally and got quite angry. After the date was finally over, I went home and lay down on my bed and cried myself to sleep.

When I turned sixteen, I decided to stop the foolish facade and accept myself completely. It was hard. I live in a small city with narrow-minded people, and there was no one to open up to. I think I really matured mentally during this stage and, of course, had all of this bottled up inside me while I really yearned to tell someone. I thought about telling my family, but they would never understand; none of my friends were capable of understanding either. Who could I turn to? My last hope was God. I poured it all out to Him, asking Him if I was weird or perverted or, worst of all, if homosexuality was a sin. Although I never received a direct answer from Him, I came close to Him and felt very good after I "talked" to Him.

I started my junior year in high school with renewed confidence in myself. I came very close to God, and we shared a mutual love. About this time, I met a really nice young man about my age. We had most of our classes together, and we became close friends during the last few months of school. I never thought of mentioning to him that I was gay, though, at least not then. His opinion of gays was very negative; some of his harsh words when I would casually mention the subject included "cocksuckers," "faggots," and "queers." He talked of them with utter disgust. This really hurt my insides, and I was having to live the kind of life I detested – one of make-believe.

After we'd became close, he decided that he wanted to get a post office box so that he could get mail that he didn't want sent to his home. I agreed on this, and we got a box together. About this time, I had met a wonderful man on the staff of the *Gay Community News,* and he had been corresponding with me. My mail from him was being censored at home, so I thought no harm could be done by receiving some letters from him at the box. My friend was a curious little fellow, and I received a package one day that was torn at the edges. He didn't think any real harm could be done by opening the package, so he did. The package contained some books on gay youth that I had ordered. Now the cat was out of the bag.

He asked me about it, and I decided to stop denying it. I came out to my best friend. I told him that I was homosexual and that I was receiving literature about it. At this stage in my life, it is still too painful to discuss the consequences of his rejection. I haven't gotten over the loss of my friend yet, and I probably never will. But I've learned some real valuable lessons about life, and I've learned them early enough, I hope, to prevent any further losses. I've learned that people are unique in their own peculiar ways, and I learned that most people are more readily able to accept old ways than they are able to accept new ones.

I could go on and discuss the loss of my friend, the painful nights crying and wondering, the disgusted looks he gave me at school, and the fact that I had to face pain too early. But why should I tell what each person has to learn by himself? That is really the sad part about all of it: we are expected to hold so much weight on our shoulders and then to try to live life like everyone else. Everyone experiences pain, the emptiness of losing someone you love very much. But why should we be tormented and ridiculed? There are so many unanswered questions. Maybe someday, someone will realize what a ridiculous predicament society puts homosexuals in. Until then, I guess we must keep the faith and never stop fighting. I firmly believe that *everyone* will experience total happiness – it may only be for one minute of one day, but everyone will know what it's like to be happy, free, and independent. *Shalom.*

Kozie, 18

Concord, California

I'm eighteen years old and gay. I've always liked looking at girls, but I never told anyone, because I hoped I would grow out of it. When I was about thirteen, around when *Charlie's Angels* came out, I fell in love with Kate Jackson. I thought I'd grow out of it. I didn't; my gay feelings keep getting stronger and stronger.

The first real gay person I ever knew was a friend, Justin. One day he walked up to me and said, "I'm gay." I didn't believe him at first, because I've known him for years and he always had lots of girlfriends.

One night Justin asked me to go to *The Rocky Horror Picture Show*. (In case you don't know, lots of gay and "bi" people go there.) I went and it was fun. I started going and getting to know everyone there. One night I went to *Rocky* just a little drunk, because we had gone to a party beforehand. I was in the lobby talking to some friends, and this girl that I really liked walked in. She came over, said, "Hi," and asked if we could talk. I went with her. As we walked into the movie, she said, "How have you been doing?" I said, "Fine, how about you?" Then we stopped walking, and she turned and started kissing me. I started kissing back. A girl that goes to my school saw us, and I was scared that she was going to tell people about Jeni and me.

When I went to school on Monday, I thought everyone knew. I was getting strange looks from people in my first-period class. When I walked into second period, everyone's eyes were on me. I didn't know what to do. I just stood there for a minute, and then I went and sat down. After class we had brunch. I went over to all the friends I hang around with. There were six of them. I came over and five of them just got up and walked away. Only one friend was left sitting there.

"What's going on? All day people have been looking at me and pointing."

"There's a rumor going around that you were seen kissing a girl Friday night."

"So that's it. It didn't take Peggy long to tell the world."

"Well, is it true?"

"Yes, it's true, I'm gay."

"Oh."

"Does it matter?"

"Not in the least."

Out of all my straight friends, Diana was the only one who stayed my friend. She started going to see *Rocky,* and after a while, she came out to me and now we're lovers.

I am out to all my friends. Mom and Dad know, but they never talk about it – well, at least not around me or Diana. I hang around with gay friends now, because I can be myself around them and show my feelings for Di and no one will look at us and say, "Look at the queers." I still go to *Rocky,* because you can be yourself there, not what people say you should be. Also, I don't have to sneak to kiss Diana. All week long, I act straight at work and at school. But on Friday night, I let it all hang out and party with the woman I love.

Robin, 16

Ohio

Ifirst heard the word "lesbian" when I was seven or eight. I had been spending the weekend over at my aunt and uncle's house, and we had all gone to the store. While they were shopping, I was browsing the magazine rack. I came across a magazine with a picture of a beautiful woman on the cover, and the word "lesbian" printed across the top. For some reason the magazine grabbed my attention, and I asked my aunt what "lesbian" meant. After she stopped laughing, she told me, "A lesbian is a woman who likes other women in *that way.*" Her tone of voice made it clear that it was a nasty and sick thing. Being young and impressionable, I believed her.

My only other source of information about gays was another uncle. He was openly gay. He was very loud, very effeminate, and always wore heavy perfume. He was the outcast of the family. Everyone was civil to his face, but they talked viciously about him behind his back. I thought he was really weird, and I avoided him.

These impressions are what caused me to panic when, at age twelve, I thought I had an unusual interest in women. Although I was young, I was not dumb, and knew exactly what my feelings meant. But I didn't put a name to it. All I had heard about gays was how abnormal they were, and that they were lesser human beings. Though there was little or no talk about gays around my friends and family (my uncle had stopped coming around), I knew what the consensus was. And then there were my own feelings about it: I believed all the things I'd been told. So I hid from myself.

At first, I told myself I was simply admiring other women's clothes, or how pretty they were; there was nothing unnatural about that. But that didn't hold up for long. Like I said, I wasn't dumb; as I got older, I couldn't believe such a dumb lie, no matter how much I wanted to. I decided to educate myself. By that time, my friends and I had talked about sex and I'd heard a bunch of terms, including *homosexual* and *bisexual*. I looked both words up in the dictionary and decided it was far better to be a bisexual than a homosexual. At least that meant I was still interested in guys. So I labeled myself "bi."

I'm sixteen now. I don't know how it happened – I can't give a step-by-step account – but somewhere along the way, I shed "bi" and took on "lesbian." I don't know why. I didn't read a self-affirmation book. There were no role models (gay or otherwise) that came into my life and made me feel better about myself. I guess I just decided I had to live with it. I went through a period in my life where I faced my differences (and there are many) and accepted them. I came to know myself, and I'm proud of who I am.

I've begun to educate myself on homosexuality. I'm reading books on gay and lesbian teens. Though I'd never dwelt on it, I realize now that I often felt I was the only gay teen. Now, whenever I'm in a room full of teens or at school, it helps to think of the one-in-ten statistic and know that there's someone like me nearby.

I found lesbian romance books at the main branch of the library, but I'm still nervous whenever I check them out. I always hope the librarian won't notice what kind of books they are. I've been reading feminist books and lesbian poetry.

And I took a huge step toward acceptance of my lesbianism: I finally got up the courage to attend a meeting of PRYSM (Presence and Respect for Youth in a Sexual Minority). PRYSM is a sort of support group for lesbians and gays aged twenty-two and under. I'd always wanted to go, but I was afraid of what the people there would think of me. (I'm sort of low in the self-esteem department sometimes.) At the meeting, all my past perceptions were challenged; it wasn't so much what was said, but the people themselves. All the stereotypes I'd had about gay males went down the tubes. I would never have guessed that some of the guys there were gay. That meeting was the catalyst for my new life as a lesbian. I've seen gay people at the library in the gay book section; before the meeting, I'd never *noticed* anyone. Of course, I knew I wasn't the only person who checked those books out, but it was like I'd developed a new awareness.

At the first meeting, a man asked me if I was bi or lesbian. It threw me off guard, but without missing a beat, I told him I was a lesbian. That was no small potatoes for me. I had never said it out loud to anyone. The experience of admitting my sexuality to a stranger gave me courage. Now, I check out romance novels without a blink at the front desk, and I'm going to buy some buttons to put on my jacket. The other kids at the meeting also gave me the courage to stop trying to hide who I am. Many of them are out at their schools.

I've only told one other person about my being a lesbian. He's my best friend. I told him because, although his opinion of gay males isn't that great, he thinks lesbians are cool. (He wants one for a girlfriend. I haven't pointed out to him that I doubt a lesbian would want to be his girlfriend.) It isn't the best support, but it is support.

Other than that, no one knows. I think a few people suspect, but they haven't said anything. There are times when I feel an immense urge to just tell people, but then my common sense gets the better of me – or, rather, my fear gets the better of me. I imagine the stares and the whispers. I'm not real close friends with any girls, but I can see them getting nervous around me, even scared. I can imagine a session in the guidance counselor's office, and maybe a phone call to my mother.

My mother is the last person I would tell. We're not close and probably never will be. I'm not even sure I'll keep in contact with her once I move out. I would feel entirely uncomfortable facing her – or anyone – if she knew. I'm not ashamed of being gay anymore, nor do I pretend to be interested in guys. But I have not yet reached the point where I can shout it to the world. It has nothing to do with my sexuality; it's simply that my self-confidence is quite low.

Sometimes I still find myself slipping back into that old frame of mind. I call girls I don't like "dykes" and guys I don't like "fags" and "queers." It's not a conscious put-down of homosexuals; that would be hypocritical. It's just that I've learned to associate these words with things I don't like. It'll take time to erase all that conditioning. I find myself making fun of effeminate males, and saying to myself, "God, what a queer!" Then I stop and say to myself, "Well, *you*'ve got a nerve." I'm trying hard to stop this thinking, because I don't want to be like Roy Cohn and lash out at gays to hide my own homosexuality.

At the same time, though, I do find myself defending gays when I hear us attacked in school, even when it's done by my friends. They are very close-minded about homosexuals, and I'm trying to rid them of the stereotypes they fell prey to, just like PRYSM quickly relieved me of mine. I'm coming to terms with my lesbianism, and sometimes feel a surge of pride. I feel quite comfortable around gay men, and I've noticed that I don't have the urge to make fun of anyone. I often feel the urge to just be around other gay people; I feel I belong there. I've rarely felt I belonged anywhere.

It's not easy being a gay teen: dating is hard. I haven't even been in a relationship yet. There are times when I feel frustrated by people's attitudes. But now that I'm accepting who and what I am, I wouldn't change it for the world.

Mike Friedman, 17

St. Paul, Minnesota

My name is Mike Friedman, and I would like to relate a few of the experiences that I have had over the last few months, because I think they might be of use to people who are in the same position.

Last summer, I finally came to grips with the fact that I was gay. I had been having sex with a man since I was fourteen, but I thought that it was just a phase that I was going through. I thought that I would grow out of it, but I obviously didn't. Last summer, I decided that I should stop kidding myself. I was gay, and I should be happy with the way I am.

I started going out to the one gay bar in our town, and ended up spending a lot of my free time there, especially on weekend nights. I found this to be rather boring after a while and stopped going to the bar, except for a couple of times a month.

At the end of August, I left home in Illinois to go to a small, Catholic, liberal arts school in St. Paul. I had thought many times about coming out to a couple of my straight friends, Brian and Richard. But I was afraid they wouldn't handle it well, and after some thought, I wasn't sure I was comfortable enough with it myself to tell someone who was straight.

The attitude of the school administration is that there are no gay students at St. Thomas. The president of the school, a priest, has been quoted as saying this in public, and the students treat gay people badly. "Fag" jokes are rampant, especially among the males. A friend of mine used to go to St. Thomas. He was in the seminary, and is now studying to be an MCC minister. He once said, "I've often wondered how many guys go back to their dorm at night and cry in the pillow because their roommate is a hunk." Amen.

I ended up living off campus and spending a very lonely fall semester. It seemed like I had no one to talk to. My roommate was straight and fourteen years older than me, so we really didn't have much in common. At the beginning of December, I decided it was time to come out to my straight friends.

Richard goes to school in Boston. Knowing that I would see him at Christmas, I wrote him a letter, and in the letter I came out to him. I didn't really know how he would react, but I thought of him as a rather liberal person in general.

I got home for Christmas and found out that he would not be home until the third week in January, and I hadn't yet heard from him. He is not a very good letter writer, so I didn't think a whole lot about it. The day he arrived in town, I spent some time with him, but he didn't bring it up, and I really didn't know how to. He was in town for only three days before he was supposed to leave for Boston. So, the night before he was supposed to leave, we went out and had some pizza and beer, and went to a movie afterward. After the movie, my sister and Richard and I were sitting around talking, and I finally brought it up. I asked him if he'd gotten the letter I had sent him. He said yes, and I asked him if there were any questions he wanted to ask me about it.

The three of us sat around and talked for two and a half hours about it. He was very supportive, and told me that he admired my guts for telling him in a letter, not knowing how he'd react. All in all, it was a very good experience for both of us. He even told me that someone had tried to pick him up on the beach in Hawaii, where he'd been just before coming home.

He told me that someone had been near him all day, and kept looking over at him all day. I told him, "You were being cruised."

"What?"

"You were being cruised."

I just laughed. Richard did not think it was as funny as I did. I told him he should be flattered. He admitted to me that he was, but wasn't interested. The guy had even asked him to go out with him that night. Richard went, but only after telling the guy he wasn't interested. I still think back on his telling me that, and laugh. I will admit that I don't blame the man – Richard is quite attractive.

When you come out to friends who are straight (or at least who you think are straight), you should tell them, and then get them to talk about it. Straight people have a lot of misconceptions about gays. Even so-called liberated people still have these misconceptions. If they react in an adverse way, try to explain to them that it doesn't change you in any way. You're not a different person just because you are gay. Then tell them that it really is no business of theirs whom you go to bed with, but that you wanted to share with them an important part of your life because they are your friend.

First and foremost, remember that you are an individual; unique, different from everyone else. Being gay is a good thing. Don't let anyone tell you that it is a sin to simply be yourself. No one chooses to be gay, it is just the way we are.

Aaron Fricke, 19

Cumberland, Rhode Island

I cannot remember a day in my life when I did not have sexual feelings. Since the dawn of my memory, I can remember not only being sexually aware but also being sexually active to a certain degree. As a child I idolized GI Joe dolls. I would undress them and look at them. I first became sexually active with my playmates when I was five or six, but I was never the first to initiate anything. What we did seems primitive now, but actually it isn't as childish as it seems. We were human beings who had no social inhibitions and were willing to explore our sexuality to its fullest extent. My friends were always boys, and if pressured into giving a reason for my homosexuality, this is the only one I can come up with. But I don't think the cause-and-effect relationship is really that simple.

I managed to avoid contracting venereal disease through all of my toddler and preteen years. In fourth grade, I had my first confrontation with the Cumberland school system. For some reason, I decided to kiss some of my acquaintances in the public schoolyard. Nothing prominent really, just a peck on the cheek. The students immediately ran to the guard on duty or to the teacher and told of the atrocity that had been perpetrated upon them. The whole thing was sort of a twisted version of the Georgie Porgie nursery rhyme. The episode was reported to the principal. He held a conference with my mother and told her that her nine-year-old son was a homosexual. I had heard the word "homosexual" before and had a general idea of what it meant, but this was the first time I had heard it applied to me. I'll always remember the petrified look on her face when my mother discussed it; it left me feeling that the subject was unpleasant.

From early childhood, my sex life continued fervently for years without disruption. When I was twelve, I began to detect a sense of guilt from my partners. I felt many times that I got the cold shoulder following sex. It began to spread to other times. Slowly, my friendships with people I had been close to all my life began to dissolve.

This was the beginning of a tumultuous adolescence. Things got worse. I felt isolated, estranged; I had no one to relate to. I had no literature to read. I knew no one who would tell me that there were books that supported gay rights. I knew of no gay organizations. (There were none in Cumberland, and there still aren't.) My self-esteem plummeted. I found it impossible to confide in anyone about my inner feelings, and that made it all the more difficult to cope with my emotions. Sometimes I would get fearful that someone might uncover my secret. I became paranoid – not only of other people but of myself and my own feelings. I tried desperately to deny my true thoughts. My entire life was one of utter confusion.

I became withdrawn. I had no means of expression. My school grades dropped, and I retreated into a life of nonstop eating and listening to the radio. In seventh grade, I weighed 140 pounds; by eleventh grade, I weighed 217 $^1/_2$ and spent eleven hours a day listening to the radio. I had trouble dealing with the outside world. And every day I lived in fear that there was nothing else, that I would never know anyone who could understand me and my feelings.

In the eleventh grade, I met Paul Guilbert. Paul was open with me about his sexuality almost immediately when we met. I found it an incredible revelation. I had been harboring many feelings inside for years and years, and now someone was telling me, very casually, "Oh yeah, I'm gay." I wanted to scream and holler and jump up and down, but I handled it much more discreetly, saying, "Really ... well, even though I'm straight it doesn't bother me." I was very paranoid at the time. Living in a shell for years does that to a person. It took a few weeks before I was able to feel secure enough to trust Paul with the horrible secret I had been concealing for so long. Paul taught me that it was not a horrible secret, that it was merely a matter of individuality and nothing more. My feelings about myself soon changed dramatically. I didn't feel any self-pity; I felt anger. I wanted to strangle the entire straight world for making adolescence, which is hard enough for most people anyway, so much harder for people like me. I think I will always carry the scars of the mental vacuum I had been kept in during my teenage years.

Paul introduced me to many of his friends. Most of them were gay, and I found it fulfilling to be able to share my feelings. I had never expected to be able to talk about those feelings to people who would still treat me as an individual. I no longer had to sit in my room and eat voraciously to lose touch with my feelings. I could share them with someone. There was no secret to be kept anymore. I didn't have to harbor paranoid feelings anymore, because there was nothing to fear. It was okay to be gay, okay to be different. And being different didn't mean a life of loneliness and solitude. I learned that my friends and I could be different together. I was not merely out of the closet, I was out of the coffin.

Editor's note: Aaron Fricke went on to make national news in the spring of 1980, when he took Paul Guilbert to his senior prom. He tells his full story in Reflections of a Rock Lobster: A story about growing up gay, *which was written in the year following his graduation.*

Kris Bowles, 19
Jinks, 19

Ogden, Utah

Kris: All my life I've noticed I had feelings for women. I had feelings for guys too. I had a few boyfriends in high school, but it just didn't feel right. I didn't love them or really even like the thought of hugging or kissing them.

Then one day, I met Jinks. I thought she was kinda cute; she had beautiful green eyes. Anyway, we had a lot in common. We both liked wrestling and the same kind of music. We cruised the boulevard and did crazy things like that. We became the best of friends. In January, she moved into my mother's house to live with me.

We slept in the same bed, and I really enjoyed having her by my side. I knew I cared more about her than about any of my other friends. Really, I loved her. But I knew it was wrong to feel that way about another girl. At the time, I hadn't admitted to myself who I was. So I tried to ignore my feelings. But they continued to grow.

Little did I know she felt the same. It wasn't until March that we confessed our feelings for each other. That night for the first time, I felt love. When we started to kiss, I got a tingling sensation all through my body. It really felt good to be touched by her and to finally be able to touch her. For the first time, it felt "right." It felt wonderful to finally know who I was – a lesbian. I felt like a great weight had been lifted off me.

The problem was that I had to tell my family and friends. I waited a couple of months. I thought for sure my mom would disown me or kick Jinks and me out of the house. To my surprise, she just hugged me and told me she still loved me. And she didn't hate Jinks either. She did say that she didn't approve of my "lifestyle." But she said it was my life to live, not hers. And that if I was happy, then that was all that mattered.

I am very happy with Jinks, but it hasn't always been easy. We had this close friend – she was the one who introduced us. When she found out, she wouldn't talk to us anymore. She wouldn't even look at us.

All my other friends have been very understanding and supportive; they still treat me the same. I'm lucky to have a family who accepts it and didn't send me to a shrink to be "fixed." I like who I am. I'm proud to be me, and I love Jinks very much. And that's *all* that matters.

I hope that every gay or lesbian out there understands that they are not alone. And that they are someone very special. Hang in there – even though everyone won't understand. It's okay to be gay or lesbian. There is *nothing* wrong with it.

▼

Jinks: Ever since I was little, I enjoyed looking at women. I would fantasize about being grown up and being with women. Lots of women!

As I got older, I really didn't know what "lesbians" were or what being "gay" was. I only knew I liked having girlfriends around a lot more than I liked having boyfriends around. I was always a tomboy, so I got along with boys okay, but I really preferred being with girls.

I had boyfriends in junior high and high school, but there was nothing – no feelings, no emotions. I even had sex with a few of them, but it just wasn't right.

When I was sixteen, I knew my feelings for women were more than just fantasies. I met a girl named Shelley. We got very close, but never did anything more than kiss. I tried other relationships with both boys and girls, but they didn't work out.

Then I met Kris, and within four months I knew I loved her. I moved into her house in January. My feelings for her grew stronger and stronger. I didn't know it, but she liked me too. After a couple of months, I loved her so much that I felt that I should move out. It was tearing me apart inside.

Finally, in March, I spilled my guts out to her. And she told me it was okay, because she loved me too. We stayed up all night kissing. It felt so good to touch her. I was ecstatic. My childhood fantasy had become an adult reality.

I must admit that it hasn't been easy. We broke up after eight months, but now we're back together. And we're going to try to make it work. I love Kris with all my heart and I'd do anything to make it work. It's so beautiful – so right.

My family doesn't accept me or Kris, but I've got to be myself. And when I'm with Kris, I *can* be myself. I hope other gay people feel proud to be themselves; we're special people. I wish everyone else would realize that it shouldn't matter; love is love. It knows no age, no color, no gender. I don't care who knows about me. I am happy with Kris and with myself. I am proud to be gay. It's who I am and nothing will ever change that.

Editor's note: This book has been two years in the making, and Kris and Jinks report that they are no longer together.

Elizabeth, 16

Kansas

I can't really say when I first figured out that I was gay. I've always known that I was just a little different from most other kids. I never really seemed to act like a girl, and most of my childhood friends were boys who played with toy cars and guns, and GI Joe. I never had a problem playing with boys. I understood them. I was a major tomboy!! I was labeled a "tough girl" when I was twelve, thirteen, and fourteen. I played a lot of sports – soccer, rugby, basketball, tennis, and softball. I kept to myself and I never let anyone touch me, especially boys. I wasn't afraid to knock some boy's head off if he touched me or one of my female friends.

I wanted to protect my friends. I couldn't understand why they wanted a boyfriend when I was there. I often imagined holding their hands and being close to them in some special way. That scared me. I liked them the way they seemed to like boys. I was sure that something was very wrong with me. I wasn't afraid of boys, but I was scared out of my mind when it came to girls.

At age fourteen, I went into deep hiding. I didn't know what the closet was at the time, but when I found it, I went deep inside and locked the door behind me. I hid what I felt from the world, because I knew people would think that I was sick and that I needed help. SHAME. FAILURE. These words passed through my head every day ... along with others that weren't so pleasant. I thought that it might be a strange phase. I didn't have a word for the way I felt. "Different" wasn't good enough for me. I felt like I was the only person in the world who ever thought of being with someone of the same sex. I thought it was wrong to imagine myself with a friend in intimate situations. It made me a "pervert" in society's eyes. I was angry that I turned out this way. I knew my feelings weren't normal. I was very afraid. I kept hoping that I would wake up one day and be boy-crazy. It never happened.

When I finally figured out what gay was, and that there was no way out of it, I cried. I saw myself as this terrible thing that nobody would ever like. Nothing has ever made me hate myself as much as being gay. I went through a time when I thought suicide was the only thing that would help.

I'll be honest. I live in a small town. In Kansas, coming out is like committing suicide. So I tried to go out with guys. It didn't seem to work, though. People still thought I was gay. I got beaten up at school, and they trashed my locker. There was nothing I could do.

Then I fell in love with my best friend. I tried to tell her about it one night. I guess that was a mistake. I lost that friendship ... and many others. At school the next day, she made it seem like I had attacked her in her bedroom.

I want to know why people hate lesbians and gay men so much. No matter where you go, you'll find a bigot. I've tried very hard, but it's hard to be nice to people who call you "queer" or "dyke." It really hurts. I don't see why everyone thinks that gay people are perverts.

I went to the library to get some books on homosexuality and lesbianism. Talk about a major hassle. I couldn't find the books on the shelves. I had to go to the front desk and ask someone to get the book for me, because they hide books like that behind their front desk in a little room. I asked her why the books were hidden, and she gave me this lecture about why books on homosexuality had to be out of sight. She spoke in a loud voice and stressed the word "homosexuality." Of course people heard. I tried to check out *One Teenager in Ten,* but the librarian gave me such a hard time and asked so many questions that I finally gave up on trying to get the book. She seemed very pleased to have won that battle. When I left the library, she gave me a really dirty look. So now, every time I'm there, I return the favor.

I came out to my family ... but not on purpose. My mom was snooping around my room and found a letter that was written by a close female friend. The letter was sweet; she had used my pet nickname and there were hints that we were romantically involved. (We weren't.) All hell broke loose. My father had always said that no queer would live in his house. He calls anyone who's different a faggot. He couldn't believe that his only daughter was a dyke. That's how he saw me: a dyke.

My mother freaked. She said that it had to be some kind of a phase. She told me it would pass soon enough. I wanted to believe her, but I knew better. When it didn't go away like she hoped, my mother got really depressed and blamed herself for making me this way. She had known that I wasn't a person who liked being touched – but now I was saying I was gay. She took me to a psychiatrist and prayed for the best. She wanted the doctor to "fix" me.

My father doesn't really have much to say to me. When I'm around, he always gets in a good gay joke or two just for laughs. He puts dykes down the most. He thinks they're just trying to prove a point and says they do "God-awful" things to each other. I am no longer my father's little girl. I honestly believe that I am nothing to him. I never knew that I could feel this alone inside.

I've lost the support of my family and my friends. I can try hard to make new friends, but my family is lost. Coming out didn't feel like a good move. In fact, it felt like the worst thing I could have done.

I can't wait to graduate and get out of this town. I just want to lead a normal life with someone I care about who truly cares about me. I've felt a lot of hate coming toward me, and it's gotten harder and harder to trust anyone. I need to know that there is hope; maybe being gay won't always be considered a terrible thing.

I'm sixteen now, and something happened recently that *proved* to me I'm gay. I stayed at an older girl's house for the night. I think she knew I was gay; I think that's why she invited me over. We were talking, and I told her about the time I got beaten up at school, and she began to cry. So did I. I never let anyone touch me, but it seemed right when she pulled me close to her and held me. When she hugged me, I knew it was okay. She looked me in the eyes and told me to never be ashamed of who I was. Then she squeezed me in her arms and kissed me. I know for sure now that I'm gay ... and I always will be. She held my hand and talked with me all night.

I now have three other friends who think being gay is fine. They even ask questions so they can understand me a little better. I'm trying not to be so hard on myself now. It's not the end of the world; for some, coming to under-stand that you are gay is just the beginning. It's good to know that some gay teens do get the support of their family and friends. I know a lot of them wind up where I am or worse.

Editor's note: Elizabeth's mother informed me that Elizabeth attempted suicide not long after this story was written. She was hospitalized for six months; the diagnosis was schizophrenia. Her mother also let me know that during that time, both she and her husband went to therapy with their daughter and came to terms with her homosexuality. Shortly after her release from the hospital, Elizabeth killed herself by taking an overdose of her own prescription medication.

Lisa, 18

Massachusetts

I am an eighteen-year-old lesbian who recently moved to a small town in Massachusetts from a big city on the East Coast. Moving was difficult for me, because I had a lot of gay friends and I was involved with a gay youth center. The city where I had lived for eleven years was very liberal and tolerant of gays. Though I was in the closet to most of my friends at school, I felt comfortable about my sexuality because of my girlfriend, gay men friends, and the tolerant community in which I lived.

When I got situated in my new home, I observed a very conservative attitude among the people. In my new school, I found that my peers were all in cliques; people who seemed "different" in any way were social outcasts.

Of course I wanted friends, so I tried to conform. I've always been sort of eccentric in my ways, expressions, and mode of dress, so blending in with the crowd became a problem.

Soon, I started denying my sexuality. I got uptight when anyone mentioned gays, and I'd make jokes about lesbians or talk about boys. Pretty soon I was obsessed with making lewd comments about the opposite sex. I got a bad reputation for talking dirty, and I felt like a hypocrite. People thought I was a real nymphomaniac. I found myself having sex with boys to prove I wasn't gay. Maybe I was even trying to prove it to myself! I didn't enjoy having sex with boys, although there are some guys I like very much as friends.

I became very confused about my sexuality. I searched for gay places in my area, but found none. The closest place was Boston, forty miles away. I don't drive, so getting there was a problem. My parents are also very strict about letting me out of the house.

I'd do anything to meet another lesbian, but it's difficult in a small town where people tend to ridicule us.

I'm sure that there are many of us with the same problem. I hope this letter comforts people in the same situation and lets them know that others share their problem.

I'll be going to college next year. I hear that college is a better place to meet gay people...

> Much luck and love,
> Lisa

P.S. Remember, you are never alone.

Terry, 19

Salt Lake City, Utah

Coming out to my parents is a major step I have yet to accomplish due to one problem: I am the oldest of three sons and the only son able to carry on the family name. The reason: my two younger brothers are both mentally retarded. I don't want to hurt my parents by telling them about me, but at the same time, I'm hurting myself by telling them lies about having a girlfriend and leading a heterosexual life. My close friends, both gay and straight, tell me that my parents already know; they just refuse to admit it and confront me with it.

I'll admit I have given hints to my parents. I told them about the first time I went to a gay disco, and the first gay man I ever met (a promising employer). They didn't really care about the disco, except that they didn't like its location. However, the gay man caused some worry, and my mother told me to tell him that she didn't care who he slept with as long as it wasn't her oldest son. And, she warned, if that were to happen, she would disown me and see him put away. My mother also discovered that I had become fond of her *Playgirl* magazines. She never said much to me, but she did start hiding them.

Then, about six months ago, when I was still living at home, I told my parents I wanted to get my ear pierced. Dad said that pierced ears and long hair were for "hippies"; he disapproved of both. Mom said that when she saw a man with a pierced ear, she automatically thought he was telling the entire world he was as "queer as a three-dollar bill."

My parents are really quite liberal, though. For my high school graduation present, they sent me to San Francisco for a week. They said it would let me grow up. Little did they know that their son did more than just grow up. As soon as possible, I moved away from home. The tension between my parents and me was becoming too great. I was always being lectured on whom I went out with, where I went, and what time I was expected to be in. So I moved into an apartment with two gay friends.

To impress my parents, and because I wanted to, I began to make some very noticeable changes in my appearance. I started wearing jeans and more rustic clothing instead of New York designer slacks and silk shirts. And I quit wearing clogs. I also cut my hair very short. This impressed my dad beyond words. He actually told me I was beginning to look and dress like a real man should. My parents asked why I was making such obvious changes, and I told them it was the latest thing. (I could hardly tell them I was trying to look like the men in *Numbers* and *Blueboy* – a real butch look, you might say.)

Every now and then, my folks would ask me how "Rose" was getting along. Rose was supposedly the girl with whom I had lost my virginity, and whom I was steadily dating. I would tell them all was fine, and the subject would be dropped.

My relationship with my parents was improving until I had my left ear pierced. Once again, Mom lectured me on her three-dollar-queer theories. But I let it go. She filled me in on all the rumors she had heard about men with pierced ears: the left ear meant you were gay, and the right meant you were into heavy drugs, etc. But I told her it didn't matter to me what other people thought. After all, it was *my* ear.

Making a career choice has also been a difficult problem. Both of my parents hate how delicately I act. I can't stand to get my hands dirty, and it makes me ill to have to gut a fish. Just picture "Albin" from the movie *La Cage aux Folles,* only thirty years younger, and you have me. I want to be a flight attendant for an airline, but my mom told me that was a job for women or men who were pansies. But, it's my life and it's my choice.

Lately, my parents have been really quiet about my earring, but they can sense that this situation with their son is not completely over. What do you think? I hate hiding my life from them, but until I'm faced with it, I'm going to remain quiet. But how long can I go on?

▼

(The following was written one year later.)

Telling my parents was probably the most traumatic experience of my life. For the past year, I had been living my life to the fullest. I had been out to my close friends for over a year, and life was great. Then came a special event. I had been seeing a guy for about four months, and we were very close to each other. Then, unexpectedly one afternoon, he asked me to marry him. He gave me a beautiful ring, and before I knew it, my life was flashing before my eyes. Within a few weeks, we were looking at houses in various neighborhoods. The pressure was really beginning to mount. Finally, I could take no more. I had one major problem in the back of my mind. My parents did not know I was gay. News of me marrying another man would kill them. So I backed out, returned the ring, and made a commitment to wait until my parents knew. This hurt me and my fiancé. Waiting would be an eternity.

The next step: telling my parents. Mom and Dad are very mellow, and I usually find talking to them to be easy. Being closest to my mother, I waited until the two of us were alone. One thing led to another, and I finally came to it. I asked my mother if there had ever been a secret that she had kept from her parents that she wished she had shared with them. I was totally serious. She laughed and replied, "My mother would have died if I told her some of the things I had done!" She wasn't making it easy. Her cute replies and my serious attitude were not mixing.

She then added, "Have you done anything that you are ashamed of?"

"No."

"Then don't let it bother you, what other people think." I then noted we had become very quiet, but I had to continue what I had started.

"What is it you're trying to say?" she asked.

"Do you or Dad have any fear in your lives about me?"

"Only one – that you're *queer!*"

That one word *queer* stabbed me in the heart. I thought I would die; my whole world was crumbling. The next thing I knew, I was in tears. I left the house. I had to get away to be by myself. What was I to do next??

I returned to the house a few hours later, and my father had since gone out, unaware of what was happening. Mother was waiting for me. She suggested that we go for a drive to talk.

In the car, her first question was, "How could you have sex with another man?" I told her that I didn't ask about her sex life and I didn't think she should ask about mine.

"What do you do to go to bed with them – get stoned or drunk out of your mind?"

I could tell that she could not relate to me on my level. After about three hours of crying and covering the Utah countryside, we returned home. She had suggested that I go to a psychiatrist and that I needed help, but most important, she said that she would help any way she could and that she loved me very much.

During the weeks that followed, my mother went to her priest, and he told her that no matter what she thought of me, through the eyes of God, I would always be her son. I also told my father. The one phrase that I'll always remember is, "Your mother and I have no further reason to live. I don't know what the hell we have done to deserve the treatment we are getting. Terry, you were our only hope." Mother also said, "You don't know how hard this is for us, to realize that we will never have grandchildren."

I feel sad for my parents. Technically, I was their only hope, because my two younger brothers are both mentally retarded. What my relatives would think if they knew hurts my father. For as long as he can remember, his younger brother has always been considered the best of the two, and today his brother is a leading church figure and an outstanding figure in the community. His brother's children are all grown and married with herds of children, while my father has three sons whom he loves dearly but who he will never be able to honestly feel have succeeded.

Time has passed, and I have done a lot of thinking. I don't blame my parents for my being gay. I don't blame anyone, because I am proud to say to people, "I'm gay." I have nothing to be ashamed of and can honestly say so. People must live their lives as they want, not as others want.

Do not try to hide or ignore your feelings. If you are gay, be proud, and if you are straight, be proud. But most of all, make the decision: be one or the other. Living two lives will eventually take its toll on you and on those you love. Remember, it's your life and you are the one who has to be happy.

Troix-Reginald Bettencourt, 18

Lowell, Massachusetts

Before I dropped out of high school, I always felt alone and out of place. I was very popular, and everybody thought I was cool. Why did I feel so isolated?

My life was a lie. I had a girlfriend. We'd been together for three years. We were the perfect couple. Then I met Mike. He was a handsome kid with a great personality. We became the best of friends. As the months went by, I fell deeply in love with Mike. And he fell in love with me. We would tell each other how much we loved each other, and we began to express that love physically.

We never considered ourselves to be gay, because fags wore dresses and put on lipstick. So what were we doing? Why didn't we tell anyone else how we were feeling? Why did it hurt so much? God, it still hurts.

As time went on, I began to realize what was I was doing. That was it. I plunged into denial and decided to buy my girlfriend a diamond to confirm that I loved her in the way that I had been telling everyone I did.

It was my seventeenth birthday. My friends had thrown me a surprise birthday party. My girlfriend was there. So was

Mike. I don't know why, but it seemed like the perfect time to give her the diamond, right there in front of everyone. I opened the box and put it on her finger. Mike left.

The next day, I went to his house wanting to know why he left. We began to argue. He told me he loved me. I remember saying, "I know you love me, and I love you." He turned away and began to cry. I went to hug him, but he wouldn't let me touch him. He jumped off the step he was standing on and said, "You don't understand! I'm *in* love with you!" It clicked. I finally realized that we were more than just two guys who were the best of friends and who happened to have sex with each other.

I didn't know what to do. I left soon after and freaked. My parents were in the middle of a divorce, and things were really shitty at home – the perfect excuse to break up with my girlfriend. So I did. My parish priest was acting as a counselor to my parents at the time, so I decided to turn to him for help. I remember talking about things at home and about my girlfriend, but I was petrified of telling him what was going on with Mike.

I began to blow Mike off and never returned his phone calls. I think it was because I wasn't ready to deal with it. Slowly but surely, I came out to my priest. I was in shock when he said, "That's fine. It's only a part of you; it doesn't make you." He was the most supportive person I've ever met. If the cardinal ever found out how helpful my priest was, he'd probably kick him out of the church.

My priest told me about this support group in Boston where there are a lot of kids like me. He gave me all kinds of information and found me the directions. I waited two months before I got up the nerve to go. I'll never forget that first day at the Boston Alliance of Gay and Lesbian Youth (BAGLY). I must have walked up and down the street about five times until someone stopped me and asked if I was looking for BAGLY. I hesitated and said yes. He asked me my name and I lied. I said Troix. (The spelling came later on.) A few minutes later, people began crowding in front of this old building where the meetings were held. The building was being renovated that day, so we had to get on the subway to get to the community center.

Mind you, I'm not from Boston, had never been on the subway before, and had never met another gay person in my life. It was the best experience of my life! There I was in a room full of kids my own age, all talking about what it's like to be a gay teen. When the meeting was over, I remember feeling lost. I didn't want to go back to the lie I called my life.

Two days later, Mike phoned me. We began to argue. I don't know why, but I just said right out, "Mike, you're gay. I know you are." I didn't tell him I was gay, however. He flipped out. He began accusing me of lying to him. He said that I never loved him, and that I only wanted to humiliate him. By the time I told him that I was gay, and that I really did love him, he didn't believe a word I said. He hung up on me. I tried calling him back, but no one answered. A couple of days later, at the next BAGLY meeting, everyone agreed that I should just give Mike some time.

That night, Mike's parents phoned looking for him. Mike had been missing since the night that he had hung up on me. The next day, I went to look for him. I found him, but he wouldn't talk to me. I cried for days. My priest was extremely supportive and everyone at BAGLY helped a lot. Mike wound up dropping out of school with only two months left until graduation. He broke up with his girlfriend, and moved to New Hampshire to live with his uncle. I've tried to talk to him since then, but he won't talk to me. He blames everything that's ever happened to him on me and my sexuality. I wonder if he'll ever come around and talk about what it was we had together.

After that, I came out to all my friends – who didn't believe me. I came out to my parents – who never would talk about it. And I came out to my ex-girlfriend, who said, "For you to trust me enough to tell me this proves to me that you do love me." And we've been the best of friends ever since.

Three months after going to BAGLY for the first time, I became the president of the group. I became very political as a representative of gay and lesbian youth. I spoke at the Boston gay and lesbian pride march, at statewide conferences, and at public schools. I even spoke at my old high school; they invited me back to speak at graduation. My picture began to appear in the newspaper frequently.

My parents knew I was gay, but they couldn't handle all the attention that I was getting. They kicked me out. They even called the police. After cracking a few gay jokes, the police took my house key and told me to leave. Legally, my parents couldn't just throw me out, because I was seventeen. So the police advised my mom to get a restraining order. On what grounds?? Who gave a shit? I decided to save them the trouble and got out ... before I got accused of stealing or something.

I filed a discrimination complaint against the officer who'd made the jokes. I called the Department of Social Services, but they couldn't help me, because I was almost eighteen. Most of my family and friends are Portuguese immigrants or children of Portuguese immigrants. (I'm from the Azores – a territory of Portugal.) Getting involved in family matters just isn't the Portuguese thing to do. And as I had become the token Portuguese homosexual, they were all worried about what people might say about them! Being gay was one thing, but helping me out or taking me in was another.

So I turned to Boston. But I didn't know what I was going to do. I had no money. My part-time job was in Lowell. I took the train to meet a friend at North Station. The train arrived, but I was afraid to get off. What was going to happen to me? How was I going to put myself through school?

Time passed. I did find a place to stay temporarily. I won my case against the police. I got a job at the Department of Health and Hospitals as the program coordinator for the Teen Line – a statewide crisis intervention hotline. BAGLY now coordinates a housing project for gay and lesbian youth in Massachusetts. In 1993, I spoke at the national March on Washington and received the Power of One award from the Human Rights Campaign Fund. I began Northeastern University in the fall of this year.

And things changed. My mom marched with me at Gay Pride '93 in Boston. But I still carry the name "Troix" to remind myself of how afraid I was to come out and be myself. I go forward – no more secrets, no more lies. Just Troix.

The fight remains, though. After coming out and establishing a life where we feel comfortable with ourselves, we tend to forget about the isolation and loneliness. We forget about those who aren't as lucky. I made it through, but what about all the other kids who fall between the cracks? Gay kids need access to housing, jobs, education, health care, counseling, and legal support. We need the help of the adult gay community to provide these services. We can't do this on our own. I was lucky to have someone to turn to. Most kids aren't so lucky.

Gary, 17

Pennsylvania

My name is Gary. I'm seventeen years old, and I'm gay. Wow, do you realize how hard it is to say that?! I'm not sure exactly when I realized, "Hey, I'm gay," but I remember that I always felt out of place, especially in grade school. I was into "girlish" things. I was never into sports, and this is still the case today. I was often made fun of in grade school. Kids would say I was gay, and I had no idea what the word really meant. Most of my friends were and still are female. Females are great friends; I'm just not sexually attracted to them.

I became aware of my attraction to men in my early teens. I hoped it was just a phase and that my interest would soon turn to females – like "normal" guys. This didn't happen. It took me a very long time to accept this. It was just this past year when I finally accepted it for myself. I felt all alone, and sometimes I still feel alone. I didn't want to be this way, and I wondered, "Why me?" I wished that I didn't have these feelings. People often say it's unnatural and against God's will. I'm not a very religious person, but I believe in God, and of course I wouldn't want to go against His wishes. But I feel if He was truly against me, He wouldn't have made me this way. I must have been born gay for some reason.

I have many pen pals. When I was fourteen, my pen pal from Nevada came to meet me. We had become very close on paper, but the subject of homosexuality had never come up. I had my first gay "experience" with him. Although I wanted it at the time, I felt awful afterwards. I couldn't believe I'd done such a thing. Looking back now, I think I was just too young to deal with it. Afterwards, when I wanted to talk about what we had done, my pen pal insisted that he wasn't gay; he just wanted to see what it was like. Shortly after he left, we stopped writing to each other. I think the reason for this is that I was angry about what had happened, especially that we couldn't talk about it. It's been three years now, and I haven't had another "experience" since.

I felt like I needed to get in touch with somebody and had no idea where to turn. I looked in the phone book and found the address of the Gay and Lesbian Switchboard of Long Island. I wrote to them, and they told me about a support group not far from where I lived. The problem was that I had no way to get there, nobody knew about me, and I wasn't ready for it myself. By the time I was ready, my parents had decided that we were going to move. I never did get to that support group, or any others. The area I live in now is extremely rural. The closest support group is almost two hours away, which isn't very practical!

The move was difficult – adjusting to a new area, making friends – but somehow I got through it. Then I learned that my new school required showering after gym. I panicked. I didn't know what the hell I was going to do! The first few times, I didn't shower, and I got away with it, but then I got caught. I had to start showering. How would I be able to do this? Showering with a group of people I'm attracted to! What if I got aroused? That would be the worst thing that could possibly happen! Somehow, I overcame this fear. I shower now, and then glance around as I get dressed. I think to myself, there's got to be at least two other gay people in here — where the hell are they?! I still don't know!

Watching talk shows helped me realize that there are other people like me out there. I just don't know where they are. Once, there was a gay seventeen-year-old on a talk show. I couldn't believe how open and accepting he was of his sexuality. I contacted the show to find out if there was any way I could get in touch with this kid. I didn't expect anything, but to my surprise, I got a letter from him a month later. We've been corresponding ever since. He sent me a copy of *One Teenager in Ten*. He was the first person that I could really talk to about my sexuality.

Then an ironic thing happened. I've had only one girlfriend — and only because she asked me out! We never kissed and rarely saw each other. After a couple of months, I told her I didn't think we should go out anymore. She was a great person, but I didn't have the same feelings she had for me. The funny thing is, a few months later, she admitted to me that she is bisexual! I came out to her, and since then we have been closer than we ever thought we'd be!

I think my parents must be suspicious about my sexuality. After all, I've have only had one girlfriend and I'm seventeen. I just can't tell them the truth yet. From time to time, one of them will ask, "Aren't there any girls in your school that you like?" I'll either make something up or try to change the subject. Then something amazing happened. My twelve-year-old sister confided to me that she is a lesbian. A few nights later, after dinner, she came out to the whole family. I know it had to be the hardest thing she ever did, and I admire her. I don't know how she was able to do it.

I wondered then if it was the right time to tell my parents about me. But shortly after my sister came out, my father told her she was just going through a phase and it would change. He told her she should grow her hair out longer and try to dress more like a girl. He then went on to say, "Fags are disgusting. If they screw each other, they'd screw anything they could." Nope – this wasn't the time for me to come out! My father is extremely homophobic. I have no idea when I'll be able to come out my parents. What makes it harder is that I'm very close to them – especially my mother. I'm afraid that after this comes out, they'll feel differently about me. Even though I'm really not doing anything, I feel as though I'm living a lie. It's very difficult.

To this day, the only family member that knows about me is my younger sister. I don't think that my parents could handle it at this point. *Two* homosexuals in the same family?! They'd probably think they did something wrong, when they didn't do anything wrong at all. Overall, I guess they handled my sister's coming out pretty well. But from time to time, my mother will say, "I just wish she wasn't this way," or my father will say to my mother, "We have to try to change her." All I can say is, "Good luck!"

I have since come out to several pen pals that I'm close to. Oddly enough, they were all gay too. It helps to be able to "talk" about certain things, but I don't know anybody around here that is gay. It would help to be able to know people personally who feel the same way I do. I haven't met a gay person here yet (at least as far as I know, I haven't). Homophobia is the problem. Just like I don't feel I can be out of the closet, many others must feel the same way. After all, there have to be about 120 other gay or lesbian students in my school, but do I know one? No. And it's hard, because there are so many good-looking guys, and I wonder if any of them are gay. Who is? Who isn't? A few people have even asked me right out, "Are you gay?" and I've denied it.

None of my friends know about me. I'm not sure how they'd deal with it, either. I'm always hearing remarks about "queers," "fags," and "dykes." I can't stand it! Little do they know that some of the people they may be saying these things to are gay or lesbian. Just recently, in gym class, the teacher was showing us a method of shooting the basketball that involved flexing your wrist – putting your hand down. A teammate said, "Just pretend you're a fag." I felt like saying, "I don't have to." But of course, I didn't. The name-calling really does hurt sometimes. I try to not let it bother me, but it's really hard to do.

A big problem is the lack of resources for gay and lesbian teens. I'm hoping that things will get easier for us and that resources will become more readily available.

Well, although I know I can't change my feelings and have accepted myself, it doesn't mean I'm happy with it. I still get very depressed from time to time. If I could change my sexuality, I would. But I can't. This was not my choice; it's just the way I was meant to be.

Nicole, 12

Pennsylvania

My name is Nicole, and I'm a lesbian. I'm twelve years old. I know you people think I'm young, but I know how I feel. I never liked any boys. But I've liked a lot of girls. At first, I thought it was wrong, because I didn't know any other gays.

I figured out for sure that I was a lesbian this year. There's this girl that I really like. I never felt this way for any other girls. When she looked at me or when I looked at her, my heart just skipped a beat. Now we are good friends.

I came out to my big sister when I was ten. She was the first person I came out to. I was a little nervous. But she really helped me through it. She told me that I was no different. We talked for a couple of hours. She told me that she thought I should tell my mom. It was very hard for me to do. But I went into my mom's room and asked if we could talk. I told her all about me. She listened, and we talked for a while. She told me that it was probably just a phase. I wondered why everybody thinks I'm going through a phase.

A few months later, when I was eleven, I wanted to tell my older brother, Gary. My mom didn't think that was such a good idea. She said he might call me bad names when he was mad at me. But I told him. He heard me out. He told me he wasn't against gays and that he thought they were just like everyone else. That made me feel very good. I was glad I told him.

So my mom, sister, and older brother knew about me. The only people in my family that didn't know were my dad and my little five-year-old brother. I knew I couldn't tell my dad. Whenever we watched a movie, there would always be someone that was a little different. And he'd always make comments. One happened to be about a gay man. My father said, "Why's this fag on TV?" That really hurt me.

But one night last year, I asked if we could have a family meeting. I was very scared, but my mom and my sister thought I should do it, because my dad was the only one that didn't know. So, we had a family meeting. It took me awhile to say even one word.

"Dad?"

"Yeah?"

"You know how there are different people?"

He had no idea what I was talking about. "What do you mean?"

"Dad, I'm gay."

"You think you are, but you're not," he said in a calm way.

I said, "Yes, Dad, I'm gay."

He said, "No matter how you are, I will always love you."

After the family meeting, Gary called me into his room. He asked me to sit down. He told me he was very proud of me and said he had something to tell me. He said, "Nicole, I'm the same as you." I said, "You're gay too?!" I was very happy. I was so relieved to know another gay person, especially one in the family. He showed me *One Teenager in Ten*. I was very happy that he was helping me. Every now and then we talk about us. But we only talk when we're alone, because he hasn't come out to the family yet.

A few weeks later, my dad called me into his room. I thought I was going to get in trouble for being on the phone too long. He said that he loves me very much and will accept me however I am. Then he said that he hopes it's just a phase. But if I don't change, he will love me just the same.

I haven't come out to any friends yet, because they say mean stuff about us. They really don't understand about it. One day this year, I was on the phone and my friend read this article to me about a lesbian. I wondered if she was coming out to me or if she was against them. Why was she reading it to me? She finished, and then she said, "Wasn't that disgusting?" I kept silent. Then she changed the subject. I guess I'll have to accept the fact that some people dislike gays and lesbians. If you are gay, don't be ashamed. We all are humans.

Bill Andriette, 16

Levittown, New York

As a young child, I unquestioningly accepted the popular perception of homosexuals, until I discovered that I was one. That realization hit me when I was twelve, though already I had sometimes mulled over the possibility in my mind. It was not that a nascent sexual drive was emerging with my pubic hairs, but rather that I was beginning to analyze and understand the things I had keenly felt and blithely savored since age five or six.

It was a shock to discover that my impassioned, if inarticulated, love affairs with fellow schoolboys that had held so much poignant beauty carried that weighty word, *homosexual.* Armed with only the information gleaned from twelve years of living in a homophobic society, I sat with the dictionary opened to that fateful term, smarting still from having made the connection between its meaning and my feelings.

Into the dark confusion of sexual self-discovery, gay culture emerged to me as a guiding light. It not only assured me that there were others of my persuasion, it also gave a structure to what had been a shapeless mass of unsorted desires; it showed me how those desires could be confirmed, developed, and ultimately satisfied. The gay media gave me a sense of community that helped take the place of what were often inaccessible gay relationships.

Almost invariably, being gay and young puts one at odds with institutions concerned with youth. The home and school may cease to be sources of emotional support, or at least become diminished, as the young person discovers his or her inability to deal with homosexuality. Such rejection, when it does not have disastrous consequences, is motivation to explore the world beyond. It can propel the rural or suburban gay into the city, make the shy person stand up for his or her rights. It can lead to books that would have been otherwise unread, and politics that would have been left unexplored.

The young gay just coming out needs, above all, accurate information to cut through the ignorance caused by silence. If resourceful, he or she may find information in the public library available more or less anonymously. But the gutsy, down-to-earth reassurance needed will almost never be found amidst the dusty tomes the library dared to buy. And what benefit does it bring to know Gay Is Good when your peers think Homosexual Is Horrible? For gay liberation to have any value for youth, people must be reminded, preferably in fifth- or sixth-grade sex education classes, that gay is not only good, but probably a part of most sexual makeups.

Jennifer Hanrahan, 18

Milwaukee, Wisconsin

Most of the time, I call myself bisexual, but I dislike labels. They tend to box you in. My sexuality shifts from day to day. Some days I feel very gay; I'm attracted only to women. Other days I feel very straight. Some days I'm just plain confused! Overall, I'd say I'm more attracted to women than to men, at least physically.

I realized I wasn't straight about three years ago, when I found myself hopelessly infatuated with a straight girlfriend. I tried to ignore it, but I couldn't stop thinking about her. Every time I thought I might be gay, I became very scared. I didn't know any gay people (at least, I thought I didn't), and I was worried about what people would think of me.

I avoided the issue for another year. I didn't see my friend very much during that time, so it was easy to ignore the fact that I might be gay. But then I fell in love with one of my teachers — a married woman. This time I couldn't deny what I felt. I thought I must be bisexual. I certainly couldn't be straight. It scared me to death. I was obsessed with keeping it a secret. I even wrote notes in my diary in code so that no one would suspect I was one of "those people."

I was suicidal many times during that period. I had very low self-esteem. I had problems with my parents, and was getting low grades in school. I was hospitalized twice for severe depression. During my second hospital stay, I came out to my psychiatrist. He was supportive, but I could tell he didn't really understand. Straight people cannot comprehend what it's like to be gay in our society.

Around this time, I had a burning desire to tell my best friend all about me. My psychiatrist warned me that she might not take it well and could reject me. But I was prepared for anything. One cold April day, my friend and I went to a sub shop after school.

"I have something to tell you," I said, swallowing hard. I wiped my sweaty palms on my jeans.

"What? What is it?" she asked, munching on her turkey club.

"Oh God...," I stammered. "This is harder than I thought." I took a deep breath and said, "I'm gay."

"Are you in love with me?" she asked.

"Um ... no. That's not why I'm telling you."

"Oh, okay then. I don't care. It doesn't affect anything."

I breathed a sigh of relief. I still had a best friend, and she still liked me – no matter who or what I was. We're still best friends. She tells me about the cute guys at school, and I tell her about my beautiful co-worker.

After that, everything kind of snowballed. I came out to my mother the next month. My parents are divorced, and I live with my mother. She wasn't as supportive as I had hoped. She asked me questions like "How can you know that you're gay when you've never had a sexual experience?" I told her I knew inside that I wasn't straight. It's not something you decide. It just happens, and you just know it. At least my mother wasn't hostile, but it took awhile for her and my stepfather to get used to it. They don't mind it now, as long as I don't bring it up too much.

My father was a completely different story. He reacted with anger and disbelief. I've never gotten along with my father, so I didn't expect too much. He insisted that I was just being rebellious and trying to make him look like a bad father. If I was just trying to be rebellious, I wouldn't pick something that would endanger my life, turn half the nation against me, and prohibit me from serving in the military! And as for making him look like a bad father, he didn't need any help from me.

I also told my two stepsisters, ages fourteen and seventeen. They were shocked at first, but now they are fine with it. They keep asking me if I have a girlfriend yet!

I still didn't know any openly gay people, so I decided to find some. I saw an ad in the local weekly paper for an ACT UP (AIDS Coalition to Unleash Power) meeting at a local church. I had heard of ACT UP in the national news, and figured there would be gay people there. I was right. Just about everyone at the meeting was gay. I met Patrick there, and he became a good friend. I made many connections through the people that I met that night. I learned about Gay Youth Milwaukee, Queer Nation, and the Gay Lesbian Bisexual Community at the University of Wisconsin (GLBC). Over the next few months, I met many more gay people. I've learned that gays and lesbians are everywhere. It's just that many times, they're invisible. It takes searching to bring them out of the woodwork.

I went to the gay pride parade in Milwaukee. Thousands of gay people, all over the place. Loud and proud! It was incredible. Nothing made me feel better than being surrounded by all these people who were just like me. I even bumped into a few high school classmates that I didn't know were gay. And then the university held a gay and lesbian film festival. There's not much for gay and lesbian teens to do: we're not supposed to go to the bars, though many do. That's why the parade and the film festival were so important to me.

I'm still involved with ACT UP and GLBC. I have a wide network of friends who listen when I have problems with my parents or get sick of the straight world. Sometimes I get tired of being bisexual. I get sick of people calling us names, putting us down, saying we spread AIDS, and so on. I'm sick of having to lie to my grandparents: they would disown me if they found out. I cry when I think of my friends Jay and Chris, who have AIDS. Whenever I hear of someone getting fired, evicted, beat up, or killed because they are gay, I am disgusted and angry. Sometimes I just wish I was straight. I wish I was "normal" like everyone else.

But being gay and being involved in the gay community has made me a stronger person. I am not ashamed of what I am. I feel pride when I see one of "my people" in Congress; honor when I see them battling discrimination in the military; respect when my friends risk arrest to fight AIDS; and dignity when I speak to a high school group and tell them that we are people, just like them.

I want to do something for the gay community, especially gay and lesbian youth. We carry the heaviest burden. We are already dealing with everything that all teenagers have to go through. Then, on top of that, we have to deal with society's taboos against our sexuality, rejection from family and friends, gay-bashers, and AIDS. I'm surprised any of us makes it.

But I believe someday things will be better for us. They're getting better all the time. Meanwhile, we have to stay strong individually and as a community. To any young gays or bisexuals reading this: Don't listen to the lies that straight society spreads or the names they call us. To borrow an old civil rights slogan, "Gay Is Okay!" Don't let anyone else tell you different. Try to find the gay community in your area. Everything is easier with someone by your side who knows how you feel. I know what a lonely feeling growing up gay can be. But believe me, *you are not alone.*

If you work with teenagers

In compiling *One Teenager in Ten* and then *Two Teenagers in Twenty,* I've had a chance to compare the experiences of gay and lesbian teens over a period spanning almost fifteen years.

When Sasha Alyson and I decided to update the book, we hoped that in the years since work began on *One Teenager in Ten,* things would have gotten a little better for gay teens. Sadly, that was not the case. In 1993, *more* of the kids with whom I corresponded were talking about suicide than had done so a decade earlier. Several had already tried to kill themselves, some more than once. Elizabeth – one of the kids who shared her story with me – did not live to see it published in this book.

These stories make it clear: the isolation and self-hatred that our society imposes on gay teenagers can kill them. Many kids know they're gay or lesbian for years before they dare mention it to anyone. Even if they know of a gay bookstore or a teen support group, they typically can't or don't dare go there. But during those difficult years, they're in school every day. They come to your classes. They use your library. They play on your team. They go to your church.

You can reach out to them. You don't have to be able to identify them; you can do it by talking to all the kids. Stop students who are making fun of "faggots"; let them know that you don't tolerate bigotry of any kind. Even one comment like that can mean a great deal to an isolated teenager. Buy books with gay and lesbian themes; some suggested titles appear at the back of this book. Place those books where they can be perused easily and privately. Post flyers from all kinds of support groups – and include flyers about gay hotlines and support groups. Put them in a place with other notices ... so that it's safe to stop and read.

It can be that easy. You're not recruiting. You're not even advocating. You're simply saving lives.

More reading

Check with your local bookstore or library for these books. Many stores now have a gay and lesbian section, and most larger cities have a bookstore that specializes in gay literature.

Fiction

Annie on My Mind, by Nancy Garden. Liza and Annie's friendship grows into a relationship of attraction and love in this novel, which is among the best of its kind.

Better Angel, by Richard Meeker. This wonderful novel, first published in 1933, is still a memorable and moving coming-out story.

Choices, by Nancy Toder. A classic story of lesbian love and identity.

Consenting Adult, by Laura Z. Hobson. A young man comes out to his parents, and his mother must learn to accept the news.

Crush, by Jane Futcher. In her senior year at a girls' school, Jinx realizes that Lexie – beautiful, popular Lexie – wants her for a friend.

The Front Runner, by Patricia Nell Warren. The story of Billy Sive, young, proud, and gay, and the nation's best Olympic hope.

Happy Endings Are All Alike, by Sandra Scoppettone. Jaret and Peggy are two high school seniors in a small town and in love with each other.

Independence Day, by B.A. Ecker. Mike falls in love with his best friend. Through the help of a teacher, he learns to deal with being gay.

Just Hold On, by Scott Bunn. Stephen and Charlotte are very close but he also has feelings toward Rolf. Together, he and Rolf explore these feelings.

Patience and Sarah, by Isabel Miller. In early-nineteenth-century New England, two women fall in love and live together. With no precedent for their relationship, they let their feelings guide them.

Ruby, by Rosa Guy. Desperately lonely, Ruby is drawn to Daphne, who is everything Ruby is not. They fill the emptiness in each other and love each other despite the knowledge that their happiness will end as abruptly as it began.

Rubyfruit Jungle, by Rita Mae Brown. Molly Bolt is a funny, reckless, and wild dirt-poor Southern girl, a full-blooded, all-American, 100 percent true-blue lesbian – and proud of it!

The Truth about Alex, by Anne Snyder. Brad finds out his best friend is gay. Brad doesn't feel this affects their relationship, but the rest of his small town disagrees.

Trying Hard to Hear You, by Sandra Scoppettone. A summer youth theater group is shattered by the revelation that two of the boys in the group are gay.

Nonfiction

About Our Children, by Parents and Friends of Lesbians and Gays. A multilingual booklet sharing the experiences of the PFLAG organization.

Another Mother Tongue: Gay Words, Gay Worlds, by Judy Grahn. This fascinating account of gay life throughout history will make you proud to be gay.

The Best Little Boy in the World, by John Reid. A moving account of one man's experiences of growing up gay, including how his brother and parents accept him and how he learns to accept himself.

Changing Bodies, Changing Lives: A Book for Teens on Sex and Relationships, by Ruth Bell. Teenagers discuss the changes and experiences they are going through, including a thorough discussion of gay teenagers.

Coming Out to Parents, by Mary V. Borhek. An exploration of the fears and misgivings that gays often have about coming out to their parents and the feelings that can beset parents when they do.

Coming Out Right, by Wes Muchmore and William Hanson. Many aspects of gay life are described for the newcomer – how to meet other gay people, what to expect at bars, health issues, and more.

Gay Sex, by Jack Hart. This illustrated manual discusses all the varieties of gay sex. It shows how you can have a satisfying and healthy gay lifestyle, without putting yourself at risk of getting AIDS.

Gayellow Pages. A directory of gay and lesbian organizations, services, bookstores, businesses, and more, in the U.S. and Canada. Updated annually.

Is the Homosexual My Neighbor? Another Christian View, by Letha Scanzoni and Virginia Ramey Mollenkott. A blending of biblical research with recent psychological and sociological findings makes this an ideal book for Christian parents.

The Lavender Couch, by Marny Hall. If you feel that therapy would help you better deal with some of the problems you face, this book will help you find – and productively work with – a good therapist.

The Lesbian Sex Book, by Wendy Caster. An informative and entertaining guide to lesbian sex that also looks at related topics such as intimacy, health, and lesbian politics.

Lesbian/Woman, by Del Martin and Phyllis Lyon. A highly personalized account of lesbian and gay rights, feminism, and an analysis of lesbian existence. An excellent introduction to what it means to be a lesbian.

My Son Eric, by Mary V. Borhek. A mother struggles to accept her gay son and discovers herself in this honest, compassionate tale.

The New Loving Someone Gay, by Don Clark. A sympathetic and perceptive guide for gays and their friends and families. One of the best books to help you love yourself or a friend who is gay.

The New Our Bodies, Our Selves, by the Boston Women's Health Collective. An excellent health resource book for women, covering lesbianism as well as other topics.

Now That You Know, by Betty Fairchild and Nancy Hayward. A challenging and enlightening guide to help parents understand what their gay children are trying to share.

Positively Gay, edited by Betty Berzon. Essays about family relationships, mental health, religion, coupling, and more.

Reflections of a Rock Lobster, by Aaron Fricke. Fricke received national attention when he took another male to his high school prom. This is his true, gripping story of growing up gay.

Revelations: Gay Male Coming-Out Stories, edited by Adrien Saks and Wayne Curtis. Personal tales of coming out from twenty-two men of very different ages and backgrounds.

Society and the Healthy Homosexual, by Dr. George Weinberg. This book, which introduced the concept of homophobia, tells how to guard against its subtle influence.

Testimonies: Lesbian Coming-Out Stories, edited by Karen Barber and Sarah Holmes. Twenty-one women of widely different backgrounds and ages describe their process of self-discovery as lesbians.

Young, Gay and Proud!, edited by Sasha Alyson. A good introduction for teenagers about what it means to be gay.

A pen pal service

Many of the contributors to this book tell how much they wanted to talk or write to someone else. In an effort to meet that need, Alyson Publications will help gay teenagers get in touch with others who would like to correspond. If you'd like to participate in this, please do the following:

1. Get an address where you can receive this mail. If you can use your home address, fine. Otherwise, some possibilities are: (a) ask at the post office how much it costs to rent a box there, or whether you can have mail addressed to you in care of General Delivery in the town where you live, and pick it up at the post office; (b) find a friend, perhaps an older gay person, who will let you use their address.

2. Write a letter introducing yourself. Be sure your address is on the letter. Put it in an envelope with a first-class postage stamp but without an address; do not seal the envelope. Then put *that* letter and envelope along with a cover letter into a larger envelope and mail it to us:

Alyson Publications
(letter exchange)
40 Plympton St.
Boston, Mass. 02118

We'll seal this letter and forward it to someone else who has expressed interest in exchanging correspondence.

In the cover letter, which will be for our confidential files, you should (a) give your name, address, age, and sex; (b) state that you are under 21; (c) give us permission to have mail sent to you; and (d) sign your name at the bottom.

3. When we get your letter, we'll forward it to someone else who has expressed interest in corresponding. We'll also keep your name on file to eventually send you someone else's letter. Once you've established correspondence with someone you should mail your letters directly to them; you'll only go through us to get that initial contact.

4. Be patient. It may take a while to get a first response. If no one replies, it could be that someone has received your letter but is having problems at home or for some other reason isn't able to write back. In that case, try again.

5. There's no charge for this service, but we ask that it be used only by gays, lesbians, and bisexuals under 21 years of age.

Getting in touch

A lot of times in this book we've mentioned getting in touch with gay organizations in your area. That's fine if you know of such organizations. If you don't, here are some suggestions for finding out about them:

• Check the white pages of the phone book under the words "Gay" or "Lesbian." There may be a gay hotline or gay alliance or similar group listed.

• Check the "Social Service Organizations" listing in the yellow pages of the phone book for gay-sounding organizations. This is a good way to find groups whose names don't start with "Gay" or "Lesbian," as well as those with clues like "Lambda" or "Lavender" in their names.

• If there's nothing in your town, try the nearest larger city. Although a group there may be too far away to be of much immediate value to you, they should know what's available where you live. Once you've explained your situation, you'll probably find them eager to help out.

• If there's any type of women's center or feminist group in town, they'll probably know of gay activities that are going on. Give them a call.

Once you've made friends with a few gays in your area, you'll find it's much easier to meet others, and to find out about gay dances, marches, bars, and whatever else you'd like to know about.

Put good books where they belong

In publishing a book like this, we face a big problem: we know that young people who are beginning to think about their sexuality need honest information about gay issues, yet it's difficult to get a book like this into the places where those young people can read it.

Many of you reading this will be in a position to help. Here's what you can do:

• After you've read several books directed at gay teenagers, ask your local library to order the ones you think are best. Many libraries will order just about any book that is requested by a patron.

• If you're a teacher – or an unusually brave student – ask your school library to also order those books.

• If you work in a youth center, make these books available there.

Other books of interest from
ALYSON PUBLICATIONS

YOUNG, GAY AND PROUD!, edited by Sasha Alyson, $4.00.
One high school student in ten is gay. Here is the first book to ever
address the needs of that often-invisible minority. It helps young
people deal with questions like: Am I really gay? What would my
friends think if I told them? Should I tell my parents? Does anybody
else feel the way I do? Other sections discuss health concerns;
sexuality; and suggestions for further reading.

THE ALYSON ALMANAC, by Alyson Publications, $10.00. The
Alyson Almanac is the most complete reference book available about
the lesbian and gay community – and also the most entertaining.
Here are brief biographies of some 300 individuals from throughout
history; a report card for every member of Congress; significant
dates from our history; addresses and phone numbers for major
organizations, bookstores, periodicals, and hotlines; and much more.
This new edition has been updated throughout. New sections include a rundown of laws and attitudes in every major country, and
a summary of major studies (from the Kinsey reports on) of sexual
orientation.

TRYING HARD TO HEAR YOU, by Sandra Scoppettone,
$8.00. Sixteen-year-old Camilla Crawford tells about a crucial sum-
mer in which her close-knit summer theater group discovers that two
of its members are gay. By the end of summer, she writes, "two of
us were going to suffer like we never had before, and none of us
would ever be the same again."

HAPPY ENDINGS ARE ALL ALIKE, by Sandra Scoppettone, $7.00. It was their last summer before college, and Jaret and Peggy were in love. But as Jaret said, "It always seems as if when something great happens, then something lousy happens soon after." Soon her worst fears turned into brute reality.

REVELATIONS, edited by Adrien Saks and Wayne Curtis, $8.00. For most gay men, one critical moment stands out as a special time in the coming-out process. It may be a special friendship, or a sexual episode, or a book or movie that communicates the right message at the right time. In *Revelations,* twenty-two men of varying ages and backgrounds give an account of this moment of truth. These tales of self-discovery will strike a chord of recognition in every gay reader.

TESTIMONIES, edited by Karen Barber and Sarah Holmes, $8.00. More than twenty women of widely varying backgrounds and ages give accounts of their journeys toward self-discovery. The stories portray these women's efforts to develop a lesbian identity, explore their sexuality, and build a community with other lesbians.

BETTER ANGEL, by Richard Meeker, $7.00. The touching story of a young man's gay awakening in the years between the world wars. Kurt Gray is a shy, bookish boy growing up in a small town in Michigan. Even at the age of thirteen, he knows that somehow he is different. Gradually, he recognizes his desire for a man's companionship and love. As a talented composer, breaking into New York's musical world, he finds the love he's sought.

COMING OUT RIGHT, by Wes Muchmore and William Hanson, $8.00. Every gay man can recall the first time he stepped into a gay bar. That difficult step often represents the transition from a life of secrecy and isolation into a world of unknowns. The transition will be easier for men who have this recently updated book. Here, many facets of gay life are spelled out for the newcomer, including: coming out at work; gay health and the AIDS crisis; and the unique problems faced by men who are coming out when they're under eighteen or over thirty.

GAY MEN AND WOMEN WHO ENRICHED THE WORLD, by Thomas Cowan, $9.00. Growing up gay in a straight culture, writes Thomas Cowan, challenges the individual in special ways. Here are lively accounts of forty personalities who have offered outstanding contributions in fields ranging from mathematics and military strategy to art, philosophy, and economics. Each chapter is amusingly illustrated with a caricature by Michael Willhoite.

REFLECTIONS OF A ROCK LOBSTER, by Aaron Fricke, $7.00. Guess who's coming to the prom! Aaron Fricke made national news by taking a male date to his high school prom. Yet for the first sixteen years of his life, Fricke had closely guarded the secret of his homosexuality. Here, told with insight and humor, is his story about growing up gay, about realizing that he was different, and about how he ultimately developed a positive gay identity in spite of the prejudice around him.

CHOICES, by Nancy Toder, $9.00. Lesbian love can bring joy and passion; it can also bring conflicts. In this straightforward, sensitive novel, Nancy Toder conveys the fear and confusion of a woman coming to terms with her sexual and emotional attraction to other women.

ACT WELL YOUR PART, by Don Sakers, $6.00. When Keith Graff moves with his mother to a new town, he feels like the new kid who doesn't fit in. He hates his new high school and wants only to move back to where his old friends still live. Then he joins the school's drama club, meets the boyishly cute Bran Davenport ... and falls in love. This gay young adult romance will appeal both to teenagers and to adult gay men who want a glimpse of what their adolescent years might have been.

BUTCH, by Jay Rayn, $8.00. Michaeline "Mike" Landetti doesn't have a word for what she is, but from the beginning of memory she has played ball with the boys, and fallen in love with the girls. Jay Rayn has written a moving story about growing up butch and learning to make your way in a less-than-accepting world. Originally published by Free Women Press.

CRUSH, by Jane Futcher, $8.00. It wasn't easy fitting in at an exclusive girls' school like Huntington Hill. But in her senior year, Jinx finally felt as if she belonged. Lexie – beautiful, popular Lexie – wanted her for a friend. Jinx knew she had a big crush on Lexie, and she knew she had to do something to make it go away. But Lexie had other plans. And Lexie always got her way.

BECOMING VISIBLE, edited by Kevin Jennings, $10.00. Drawing from both primary and secondary sources, this reader covers over 2000 years of history and a diverse range of cultures. Designed for classroom use, *Becoming Visible* contains classroom activities and curriculum suggestions to help teachers incorporate this material into existing classes. The readings are suitable for age levels from ninth grade through college, but the book will also be welcomed by general readers seeking insight into gay and lesbian history.

BROTHER TO BROTHER, edited by Essex Hemphill, $9.00. Black activist and poet Essex Hemphill has carried on in the footsteps of the late Joseph Beam (editor of *In the Life*) with this new anthology of fiction, essays, and poetry by black gay men. Contributors include Assoto Saint, Craig G. Harris, Melvin Dixon, Marlon Riggs, and many newer writers.

GAY SEX, by Jack Hart, $15.00. Today's gay man faces a very different world than his predecessor did. This lively, illustrated guide will appeal to all gay men, but especially to those just coming out. The entries cover everything from "Dating" to "Dildoes," from "Finding a Lover" to "Frottage," and all the steps in between.

THE LESBIAN SEX BOOK, by Wendy Caster, $15.00. Informative, entertaining, and attractively illustrated, this handbook is the lesbian sex guide for the nineties. Dealing with such sex practices as cunnilingus, masturbation, and penetration, as well as related topics such as intimacy, nonmonogamy, health, and political correctness, *The Lesbian Sex Book* offers the reader a potpourri of helpful advice. Never judgmental, this guide is perfect for the newly out and the eternally curious.

SOCIETY AND THE HEALTHY HOMOSEXUAL, by George Weinberg, $8.00. Rarely has anyone communicated so much in a single word, as Dr. George Weinberg did when he introduced the term *homophobia* to a wide audience. With a single stroke of the pen, he turned the tables on centuries of prejudice. Homosexuality is healthy, said Weinberg: homophobia is a sickness. In this pioneering book, Weinberg examines the causes of homophobia. He shows how gay people can overcome its pervasive influence to lead happy and fulfilling lives.

BI ANY OTHER NAME, edited by Loraine Hutchins and Lani Kaahumanu, $12.00. Hear the voices of over seventy women and men from all walks of life describe their lives as bisexuals. They tell their stories – personal, political, spiritual, historical – in prose, poetry, art, and essays. These are individuals who have fought prejudice from both the gay and straight communities and who have begun only recently to share their experiences. This groundbreaking anthology is an important step in the process of forming a new bisexual community.

THE MEN WITH THE PINK TRIANGLE, by Heinz Heger, $8.00. For decades, history ignored the Nazi persecution of gay people. Only with the rise of the gay movement in the 1970s did historians finally recognize that gay people, like Jews and others deemed "undesirable," suffered enormously at the hands of the Nazi regime. Of the few who survived the concentration camps, only one ever came forward to tell his story. His true account of those nightmarish years provides an important introduction to a long-forgotten chapter of gay history.

CHANGING PITCHES, by Steve Kluger, $8.00. Scotty Mackay is an American League pitcher who, at thirty-six, has to hit the come-back trail to save his all-star career. All goes well until he gets teamed up with a young catcher he detests: pretty-boy Jason Cornell. Jason has lots of teeth, poses for underwear ads, and has blue eyes ... and Scotty's favorite color is blue. By August, Scotty's got a major-league problem on his hands.

A LOTUS OF ANOTHER COLOR, edited by Rakesh Ratti, $10.00. For the first time, gay men and lesbians from India, Pakistan, and other South Asian countries recount their stories of coming out. In essays and poetry, they tell of challenging prejudice from both the South Asian and gay cultures, and they express the exhilaration of finally finding a sense of community.

ALL-AMERICAN BOYS, by Frank Mosca, $6.00. "I've known I was gay since I was thirteen. Does that surprise you? It didn't me. Actually, it was the most natural thing in the world. I thought everyone was. At least until I hit high school. That's when I finally realized all those faggot and dyke stories referred to people like me..." So begins this story of a teenage love affair that should have been simple — but wasn't.
